The ☜ W9-CYW-319

Reiki Factor

A Guide to the Authentic Usui System

This fascinating guidebook introduces the self-help approach of Reiki, which Dr. Ray has been practicing and teaching from the Reiki Center in Atlanta since 1978. In 1980, she founded the American Reiki Association. Reiki is not a religion or a cult. It is a natural healing and health maintenance art and science based on tapping the universal life energy present in all living things. It is a technique that can be used daily in any situation to restore energy and retain physical, mental, and emotional balance. Reiki originated in the Far East centuries ago and was unknown in the Western world until Dr. Ray discovered it through an elderly Japanese woman who trained Dr. Ray in the complete Reiki system.

Through numerous case histories, Dr. Ray describes how she and others have used Reiki to bring energy, peace, and contentment to many people, and to restore health. Through Reiki, new patterns of living can be established to cope with stress, to lose weight, and to become free of harmful addictions. In some cases, Reiki treatments have resulted in instantaneous healings. In others, they have helped sufferers to minimize the physical and emotional pain of dealing with chronic or terminal illnesses, including cancer.

In a particularly moving section, Dr. Ray describes the flow of energy and light she has felt in administering Reiki to people in the death and dying process.

Reiki has been used to heal cats, dogs and wild animals, and even restore health to plants. Now, this book makes knowledge and understanding of this easy-to-learn, highly effective healing technique widely available.

About the Author

Dr. Barbara Ray is a lifelong scholar of Latin and Ancient Civilizations. She holds a Ph.D. in Humanities, is a member of Phi Beta Kappa and Mensa, and is a Fulbright scholar in Art History. Dr. Ray is the most qualified authority on Reiki, both in her academic expertise about Reiki and in her extensive experience with Reiki.

A Reiki Master, she received full training as a Third Degree Reiki Initiator in 1979. One year later, she founded the American Reiki Association, Inc., a not-for-profit organization, now the American-International Reiki Association, which reflects the planetary outreach of Reiki.

Dr. Ray devotes all her time to lecturing, writing, and teaching seminars on Reiki and holistic health. As a New Age teacher and healer, she uniquely blends a seriousness of purpose with a loving sense of humor. In her words, "Healing is a process and a celebration of attaining wholeness and oneness and is your Divine birthright!"

The Reiki Factor

Dr. Barbara Ray

The Reiki Factor

A Guide to the Authentic Usui System

Barbara Ray, Ph.D.

Foreword by Elizabeth Valerius Warkentin, Ph.D.

Radiance Associates   *St. Petersburg, Florida*

First Printing, January 1983
Second Printing, September 1983
Third Printig, May 1984
Fourth Printing, Feb. 1985
Fifth Printing, June 1986

SECOND EDITION

Library of Congress Catalog Card Number 85-060675

ISBN 0-933267-00-2

Printed in the United States of America

This book is dedicated to *you*, the reader—
the seeker. May you find in it something for which
you are searching in your journey.

Contents

APPENDIXES

Foreword
to First Edition of THE REIKI FACTOR

It is a privilege to give my enthusiastic endorsement to the public presentation of Reiki Healing. In 1979 my husband* and I were fortunate to meet Dr. Barbara Ray and learn about this significant healing method. Since then we have developed much personal appreciation of the healing power of Reiki.

In March 1979, my husband had surgery for stomach cancer; it had spread to the adjacent lymph nodes. Eight months later the incision had not healed despite repeated surgical interventions. At that time we attended a lecture on Reiki Healing by Dr. Ray and we decided that John should avail himself of such treatments. Seventeen days later his incision was entirely healed. He has had no further symptoms of cancer.

We now have both attained the First and the Second Degree in the Reiki Method of Natural Healing.

My mother had surgery for cancer of the colon in August 1979, at eight-five years of age. There was lymph node involvement. Mother got her First Degree in Reiki and utilized it on herself. Through eighteen months of chemotherapy she had no hair loss and no weight loss, and her energy level remained high. We believe that her daily hour of self-administered Reiki treatments was a significant factor in her unexpectedly good recovery. Her cancer has not recurred.

Reiki Healing also helped my mother with the stress of my father's illness during the last months of their sixty years together. In January 1980, my father entered a nursing home because of the recurrence of hydrocephalus, for which he had had surgery the preceding January. He received many Reiki treatments during the ensuing two and one-half years and always felt calmed after them. I believe Reiki contributed much to his well-being in the final months and helped him to make his transition peacefully.

*John Warkentin, Ph.D., M.D.

In my own person I have repeatedly experienced the healing power of Reiki energy. Although I have not had a life-threatening illness in recent years, the stress from these past three and one-half years led to lesser illnesses and pains of various origins. These were significantly relieved or healed primarily by means of Reiki. A particular experience was when I had a very painful fall, landing heavily on my left knee. It began swelling rapidly so that the entire knee was conspicuously larger, with a special anterior protrusion the size of a large egg. Within an hour I got to the Atlanta Reiki Center where I was treated for two hours. The swelling decreased and the anterior protrusion was gone. That evening I was treated for an hour by four Reiki healers simultaneously; after that the swelling had entirely subsided. A physician who saw the knee swell immediately after I fell expected me to be on crutches for at least several days. He was amazed that same evening to see me walking with little pain and no swelling of the injured knee.

Two and one-half days ago I sprained my right ankle. My husband and I Reiki-ed it periodically for several hours and put on an Ace bandage. I could not walk without crutches, and the following morning I saw an orthopedist who found no fracture but diagnosed a severe sprain. He was very surprised at the absence of swelling in my foot and ankle. He said my ankle would have to be bandaged for two or three weeks and I would have to walk with crutches or a cane and be unable to drive for at least a week. With the help of Reiki there was never any swelling, and, today, forty-eight hours later, I am able to walk without help and am driving my car.

The foregoing personal vignettes indicate some of my experiences with the effectiveness of Reiki healing. The great variety of human diseases that can be favorably influenced or healed by the Reiki Method is very surprising and, at times, has seemed miraculous. The Reiki modality appears to operate via energy that is present around us at all times. I do not understand the precise nature of this energy. I do not know the mechanism by which the energy involved has a beneficent effect rather than a harmful one. Quite regularly pain is relieved rather than made worse; physical and emotional healing is promoted rather than hindered as a result of Reiki intervention. I do not know the limitations of Reiki healing. I am particularly mystified by the evidences of effective absentee Reiki healing, where healer and patient are separated by many miles. Finally, since this healing energy is apparently universally present, how can we understand the neglect by humankind of such a great good?

In the face of so many questions, I have only one clear response: whatever the mechanism, Reiki healing works!

I admire the courage of Dr. Ray in publishing *The Reiki Factor.* She is one of the first American masters of this method and presents a detailed statement of the present knowledge about Reiki. With integrity and dedication she is striving to make Reiki Healing widely available.

ELIZABETH VALERIUS WARKENTIN, PH.D.

July 1982

Foreword
to Second Edition of THE REIKI FACTOR

I am honored to be asked again to write this Foreword to the second edition of *The Reiki Factor.*

In August 1982, I was privileged to receive the Third Degree as a Master/Teacher of the Reiki Method of Natural Healing. This came at an opportune time. Three months later, in November, my husband was found surgically to have multiple metastatic carcinoma. He was given one to two months to live; he lived 12 more months. (Medical statistics had given him maximally 1½ years to live after his first surgery for a different cancer four years earlier.) In December, while still in the hospital, John received the Third Degree as a Reiki Master/Teacher. I believe that our being initiated as Reiki Masters helped us live through the ensuing year with a lightness that would not otherwise have been present. In addition, I believe I would have completed that following year with a bitterness and cynacism that had started within myself and which began to turn with that initiation.

From the time of his surgery, John was frequently very tired and had daily Reiki treatments from loving people in Atlanta and also absentee Reiki from people throughout the country. He also had four hours of Reiki every Saturday with two to 15 Reiki practitioners. Although he usually started these treatments feeling very tried, when they were over he often said: "That's a miracle; I feel wonderful and full of energy now." His color, too, changed from ashen-grey to healthy-looking pink.

John had had radiation therapy to shrink a tumor in his stomach, but it did not affect the metastases. He was also given a trial of chemotherapy which was unsuccessful for his type of cancer. Despite expectations, he was able to see patients again in May and it gave him great pleasure to be useful to others once more. In late September we saw a cancer specialist in Chicago who told us: "Reiki must be a wonderful thing to enable John to have the energy to make this trip and to have the energy he has for the degree of disease he evidences." John was able to work until the end of October when he became too weak to continue. Medically he was expected to be in a great deal of pain, but he was not. The only medication he took toward the end of his life was for nausea. In addition, after one blood transfusion in March, his blood counts remained well within normal ranges.

It was not only the physical plane on which John was touched by the Reiki. His dying was a process which involved his physical body and also his spiritual self. The healing which took place with the Reiki included that which appears to occur beyond the physical plane. At one time John appeared to be drowning in the fluid in his lungs. I sat next to him hearing the gurgles in his chest. I was in pain with him; he was my husband whom I loved. A friend, who is also a Reiki teacher,* came into our bedroom and started to Reiki John. She said to him: "It's beautiful, isn't it?" He opened his eyes, looked directly at her and said: "Yes!" It was as though he were telling us that over and above the physical and psychological torment we saw, he was experiencing incredible beauty. He also said: "I want to live with the Reiki forever." I was in bed with pneumonia next to John at that time. In fact, I had had pneumonia and other respiratory problems a number of times during the past stressful six years. I believe that without Reiki I would not have been able to physically or psychologically withstand the stress of those times.

John was lucid at the time of his transition. He lived his three score and ten years with love and dedication. His devotion was to God and to serving mankind. We both believe the Reiki helped his final years to be relatively pain-free and richly of service. When he made his transition, he stepped out in light on our 12th wedding anniversary, November 27, 1983. I learned through my husband's dying process that what matters is that you leave this world in light and love of God.

*Sara Schmidlin, Ph.D.

APPENDIXES

Appendix A

Questions and Answers

The questions included in this section are some of those most frequently asked of me at public lectures and in the Reiki Seminars.

What Is Reiki?

Reiki is a precise art and science of tapping and amplifying natural energy and of balancing natural energy by restoring vital energy to all levels of your being. The technique of Reiki can be used for promoting healing, wholeness, positive wellness, and health maintenance and for attaining higher consciousness. Reiki is a unique self-help technique.

What Is the American-International Reiki Association?

Founded in the summer of 1980, the American Reiki Association is the first membership organization for those who have studied Reiki. The main purposes of this association are to provide in *The Reiki Journal* an opportunity to exchange and share experiences with Reiki; to share ideas and concepts on healing, wholeness, higher conciousness, nutrition, and other related topics to promote public understanding of Reiki; to establish professional standards and a code of ethics for those practicing Reiki;

and to establish and maintain high standards of excellence in the training and certification of Reiki Master/Teachers so that the public can be assured of high-quality Reiki classes.

In early 1982, the title was expanded to the American-International Reiki Association so as to include persons studying Reiki in other countries and to reflect the planetary outreach of Reiki. The American-International Reiki Association is an IRS tax-exempt, not-for-profit organization. For further information write to:

> *The American-International Reiki Association, Inc.*
> *P.O.B. 86038*
> *St. Petersburg, FL 33738*

What Is the Origin of Reiki?

In modern times, this ancient technique was rediscovered by Dr. Mikao Usui in the late nineteenth century in Japan. Dr. Usui applied the term "Reiki," meaning universal life-force energy, to this self-help technique. This technique can be traced back many thousands of years through ancient India and into Tibet.

Who Can Learn Reiki?

The Reiki technique can be taught to virtually anyone. The age range that I have taught is from five to ninety-three years. I have taught Reiki to people of high health levels who planned to use Reiki for stress reduction, relaxation, and prevention of illness and to persons at all levels in between. I have also taught Reiki to persons in terminal phases of diseases for relaxation, pain relief, and higher consciousness growth. If for some reason an individual cannot learn to do Reiki, then relatives, friends, and therapists can easily learn to give Reiki treatments. Children can also be taught Reiki easily and can give the treatment to a parent or other family member needing help. Reiki gives a wonderful way for family members and friends to interact in a non-distressful, relaxing, nondemanding, nonintrusive, peaceful, caring, and loving manner.

Will Reiki Interfere with My Personal Religious Beliefs?

No. Reiki itself is not a religion or a cult of any kind. It is a harmless and gentle method of activating energy within you and using that natural, life-force energy in accordance with your particular needs.

Do I Have to Believe in Reiki?

No. Reiki is not a belief system nor is it a dogma or a doctrine.

Is Reiki a Form of Psychic Healing?

No. Reiki is a way of activating natural energy and applying it in a specific manner. Reiki runs through you and enhances any natural or undeveloped talents you might have. Several known psychics have studied Reiki with me and found that their psychic powers improved wonderfully.

Is Reiki an Occult Practice?

The word "occult" unfortunately has taken on certain negative connotations reflective of narrow prejudices in our culture. "Occult" means, literally, "something hidden from view." In tracing the history of Reiki, I found that this technique was sometimes hidden away and taught only to a chosen, special few, to the elite and to the aristocracy. Reiki is now available to anyone wanting to study it.

Do I Need Any Special Knowledge before I Can Take the Reiki Seminar?

No. But an openness to learning and growing helps! In the Reiki Seminar, you will be thoroughly instructed on the Reiki technique. Included in the courses offered by Reiki Seminars, Inc,[sm] is information on wholistic health and living wholeness, natural healing, and energy balancing. When you have completed the seminar, you will be able to use Reiki for yourself and for family or friends if you choose.

Will Reiki Interfere with My Medical Prescriptions and Treatments?

No. The Reiki technique can easily and successfully be combined with medical therapies and can be used with positive benefits before and after surgery. Many medical doctors have taken the Reiki training and agree that Reiki enhances the natural healing process. In addition, Reiki can be used in combination with exercise, nutrition, and other techniques and remedies.

How Often Do I Have to Do the Reiki Technique?

For the most effective benefits from Reiki, one needs to use this technique on a daily basis or at least a reasonable amount of time during each week. In the Reiki Seminar, you will be given specific directions in the use of the Reiki technique according to individual needs.

If I Take the Reiki Seminar and Then Neglect to Use It, Do I Have to Repeat the Course?

No. Once you have received the Reiki activating energy transmission and instructions on applying the technique, you have it for life. The energy does not run out but will amplify with use. I have often received letters from people who did not use the Reiki technique for as many as two years after taking the seminar. Those people have been able "to take up where they left off," so to speak, and benefit from Reiki years later.

How Would a Person Not Benefit from Reiki?

By *not using* the Reiki technique on a regular basis as instructed in the seminar. Too often people are looking for a quick solution to difficulties and diseases that took years to accumulate. Reiki is not a "gimmick" but is an effective, precise method of amplifying, directing, and using natural life-force energy—but you have to use it to get benefits! Reiki helps you to break up and transform negative habits and patterns into positive, self-renewing ones.

Is Reiki Effective in Helping to Control Addictive Habits Such As Excessive Smoking, Alcoholic Drinking, and Compulsive Overeating?

Yes. The Reiki technique helps you to unblock energy that is blocked in your physical, emotional, and mental bodies. Reiki releases the underlying distress usually associated with such addictions. The Reiki technique can also be easily used *anywhere* for a few minutes instead of smoking a cigarette, taking an alcoholic drink, or eating excessively. Doing Reiki gives you a direct, easy, safe way of building a habit toward your own positive wellness. Reiki is not a substitute for exercise and vital, natural foods.

As an Artist, How Can Reiki Benefit Me?

Reiki, itself, is cosmic, universal, life-force, light-energy. It is the very essence of life. Reiki is a special experience for each person, and it will enhance whatever talents you have in whatever ways these talents are expressed creatively for you.

Do I Have to Treat Other People with Reiki?

No. In the Reiki Seminar, you are taught how to balance your energies and heal yourself first. You are also taught how to give a Reiki treatment to someone should that need arise among friends and/or family members.

Appendix B

Autobiographical Sketch of the Author

As we journey through our lives, it often happens that we begin to awaken to a sense of ourselves as a whole, unfolding process. We go through cycles, we live through a myriad of events, situations, and relationships, and we even repeat patterns until something happens that changes us, taking us beyond the limits of our past.

Our individual lives differ in the outer context and details. We have different names, different skin tones, different friends, live in different countries, speak different languages, and express ourselves in different ways. Yet, in the essence of the life-force energy, we are connected, we are one. From the inside, we are of the same source, and in our hearts, we have a common meeting center of love and, ultimately, light.

I once thought of my life in terms of beginnings and endings. Gradually, I began to perceive of my life as an unfolding process moving along a spiraling continuum. My perspective expanded from seeing events, situations, and relationships as isolated and unrelated to seeing them as interrelated and part of a larger whole. In retrospect, I found that I had often misinterpreted events and that what had once seemed negative often turned out to be positive—perspective transforms everything!

Where did my journey to Reiki begin? In relating some of the highlights of this process, I will make no attempt to

125

interpret. I have long since learned that interpretations keep one from experiencing "what is." At times, some of the meanderings and some of the twists and turns of my life seemed disjointed, lacking in coherence, and even strange. Surely you know the feeling! By the time I was in high school, I had it all planned. Basically, the scenario was that I would go to college, major in Latin, teach Latin in high school until retirement, marry, have a family, travel, grow old, and die. Are you smiling yet—laughing even? In fact, some of that scenario did happen.

From the very first day of Latin class, I knew I would become a Latin teacher. I will never forget the experience for it had impressed me even more than I had realized at the time. When I opened the Latin book, it was as though closed gates in my memory tracts were thrown suddenly wide open. I knew *that* language! I could read it without knowing how I was doing it. Inwardly, I was experiencing a mixture of amazement, excitement, confusion, and fear. Outwardly, I did what everyone else was doing—listened and learned.

I studied Latin for four years in high school. Each step opened more channels in my memory. I did extra work, reading through text after text as well as studying Roman history. I won a scholarship to study Latin at Florida State University in Tallahassee, Florida. Selected to participate in a special honors program, I received a B.A. and an M.A. in five years, majoring in Latin, Greek, and ancient civilizations with a minor in history. I was elected to Phi Beta Kappa in my junior year. While finishing my master's degree, I met and married another graduate student.

I obtained a teaching position at the internationally known and top-ranked Melbourne High School in Melbourne, Florida. I was hired to teach Latin but instead spent the first semester teaching English literature and humanities. This was one of those twists to which I was referring.

In the late 1960s, I returned to Florida State to work on a doctorate. I had obtained an assistantship to teach Latin. Then came another twist. At the last minute, I was shifted to teaching the mythology course. I resisted but to no avail. You might be thinking that by then I would have caught on to the concept that "life is an unfolding process"—but no, not yet!

Then a startling thing happened. In the three years of teaching mythology, my life was transformed. The research I did in preparation for this class threw open the doors to a new dimension. I discovered that the "myths" of the ancients were filled with vital information and essential *keys* to the meaning and mystery of life. Freud led to Jung, and Jung led to the study of comparative mythology and to Joseph Campbell and endless books and articles, all revealing the same inner messages of these ancient myths which varied only in the outer forms of local names and places. Again and again, the knowledge of life, the essence of existence, and the keys to the "inner secrets" were revealed hidden beneath the outer trappings and the escapades of the local deities. To focus on the outer was to miss the key to the inner treasure.

It was not unusual to find alterations and modifications of these myths in their outer forms through the centuries, but, in the inner part, the essential truth was transmitted without change. I discovered that these myths connected us to our source directly from the *inside,* providing the knowledge of our cosmic connection and opening the gates of initiation to higher consciousness. Without this essential information, without this knowledge of who we are and what our essence is, we become lost in the maze of events in what seems like a meaningless, even futile life. When we lose conscious touch with our connection, with our source, we are in the dark and we become afraid.

My own course work included classics, Near Eastern ancient civilizations, Renaissance history, art history, contemporary art history, and a variety of humanities courses tracing man's intellectual, cultural, and scientific developments into modern times. In March 1970, I received an interdepartmental doctorate degree in humanities. Until 1976, I continued in a career of college teaching.

I had acquired an in-depth and extensive knowledge of

where mankind had been from ancient to contemporary times. From 1959 to 1970, I had been constantly in touch with information about our past on this planet. It was not possible to ignore an entire body of knowledge about the so-called mystery schools or ageless wisdoms prevalent for so long in Egypt, Greece, Rome, and the Near Eastern civilizations. I had also developed an academic interest in the ancient healing arts, which I have continued to pursue through these years.

In 1972, I won a Fulbright scholarship to study Renaissance and baroque art in Italy at the University of Rome, studying in Florence and Venice. For me, being in Italy was a profound, transforming experience. All the centuries were represented there comingling in an incredibly vibrant dance of modern life. While in Italy, I was able to continue my own study of the inner knowledges and healing arts which had been preserved in myths, religions, and visual, symbolic forms.

When I returned from Italy, I began an extensive investigation of various forms of energy systems and healing arts. I did some study in humanistic and transpersonal psychotherapies and also took astrology courses at Emory University. I studied and taught courses in meditation, parapsychology, and a wide variety of healing arts and sciences including the Tibetan art of the mandala. I had become particularly involved in wholistic dimensions in healing, health, and consciousness and in the dawning of this New Age of humanity—the Age of Aquarius.

In 1976, I shifted my full attention to lecturing, private counseling, and working with healing in the area of wholistic health, wholeness, and techniques for achieving higher consciousness. In addition, I continued my search for healing and energy-balancing methods that would tap universal life-energy in the ways I had known were possible from my formal studies of antiquity.

In 1978, I took the basic course in Reiki. From my specialized academic background, I was easily able to identify Reiki as an ancient technique for tapping universal energy and for applying this natural energy for balancing, healing, wholing, and enlightening. The origins of this technique are to be found in ancient Tibet, perhaps dating more than eight thousand years ago. This knowledge was taken eventually into India, China, and Japan as well as into Egypt, Greece, and Rome. For additional information on this topic see Chapter 8, "The Origin of Reiki."

In the four years before my discovery of Reiki, I had been gaining experience in working as a healer with a number of healing and wholing techniques. In Reiki, I recognized the piece missing from those other techniques—the process of tapping, at will regardless of your state of consciousness, a higher order of energy called *ki,* universal life-force energy. I had never previously encountered a natural energy-balancing and healing method as complete and as effective as Reiki. In addition, Reiki is for maintaining health and balance as well as for attaining higher consciousness, spiritual growth, and, ultimately, enlightenment.

I continued my study of Reiki until becoming a Reiki Master. Having found such a remarkable technique, which had been passed in various forms through the centuries, I wanted to be able to teach Reiki to others. During the last two years of her life, Hawayo Takata taught me the complete Reiki system and carefully instructed me in the advanced levels of Reiki. What I learned enabled me to validate Reiki and its ancient origins with additional certainty.

In 1979, I opened the Reiki Center in Atlanta, Georgia, and began keeping records of my healing and wholing work with Reiki. The extensive experience I obtained from working long hours as a Reiki therapist has given me the necessary practical knowledge of Reiki as a natural energy-balancing art and science. I also gained and continue to gain deep insights and sensitivity to the entire healing, wholing, and personal transformation process. Such knowledge can come only from extensive, direct experiences in working with myself and with many others. In this book, you, the reader, have the combined benefit both of my academic expertise as to what Reiki is and of my proficiency and insights obtained from my continuing practice as a Reiki therapist/healer.

In the summer of 1980, the American-International Reiki

Association was founded. Among its many purposes is providing for the public fully qualified, trained, and certified Reiki Master/ Teachers; establishing a national forum for those who have studied Reiki; and making available information about Reiki to individuals and to other organizations.

Ultimately, Reiki is not words, is not a discussion or a debate, is not a dogma or a doctrine, is not a religion, cult, or belief system, but is a direct, meaningful, and personal experience with universal life light-energy. The information I have shared in this book was intended for a wide range of individuals. If there are chapters and discussions to which you do not relate or have no interest, remember that the words can at best only describe the process and that, in the end, Reiki is an *experience*. As Einstein stated, "All knowledge about reality begins with experience and terminates in it."

For me, it is a deep honor to be able to teach others the unique and profound technique of Reiki and to work with so many people as a Reiki healing/wholing therapist so that we may all achieve our divine birthright: wellness, wholeness, and enlightenment. Ultimately, Reiki is a profound and personal experience with universal life light-energy.

Notes

1. INTRODUCTION: A NEW BEGINNING

1. William Morris (ed.), *The American Heritage Dictionary of the English Language* (Boston: Houghton Mifflin Co., 1980), p. 908.

2. Lincoln Barnett, *The Universe and Dr. Einstein* (New York: A Bantam Book, 1969), p. 108.

2. DAWNING OF A NEW AGE

1. Alvin Toffler, *The Third Wave* (New York: Bantam Books, Inc., 1981), p. 9.

2. Ibid.

3. THE WHOLISTIC MODEL

1. Harold Bloomfield and Robert Kory, *The Holistic Way to Health and Happiness* (New York: Simon and Schuster, 1978), p. 23.

2. Marilyn Ferguson, *The Aquarian Conspiracy* (Los Angeles: J. P. Tarcher, 1980), p. 85.

6. ENERGY AND REIKI

1. Jean Charon, "The Spirit: In Man . . . In Contemporary Physics" at the Second World Congress of Science and Religion, St. Petersburg Beach, Florida, June 1981.

2. Jolande Jacobi (ed.), *C. G. Jung: Psychological Reflections—a New Anthology of His Writings, 1905-1961* (Princeton: Princeton University Press, 1978), p. 30 and p. 36.

3. Quoted by Roland Gammon in the paper "Scientific Mysticism" at the Second World Congress of Science and Religion, St. Petersburg Beach, Florida, June 1981.

4. Quoted by Kay Croissant and Catherine Dees in *Continuum—the Immortality Principle* (San Bernardino: Franklin Press, 1978), p. 35.

7. REIKI: A SCIENCE OF LIGHT

1. Ferguson, *The Aquarian Conspiracy*, p. 102.

2. Ibid., p. 32.

NOTES

3. John Ott, *Health and Light* (New York: Pocket Books, 1976), p. 19.

4. Ibid., p. 192.

5. Ibid., p. 21.

6. Albert Einstein and Leopold Infeld, *The Evolution of Physics* (New York: Simon and Schuster, 1938), p. 31.

7. Carl Sagan, *Cosmos* (New York: Random House, 1980), p. 345.

10. STRESS, RELAXATION, AND REIKI

1. Hans Selye, *Stress Without Distress* (New York: Signet, 1975), p. 14.

2. Simonton, Carl, *Getting Well Again* (New York: Bantam Books, 1978), p. 44.

3. Quoted by Steven Halpern in *Tuning the Human Instrument* (Belmont: Spectrum Research Institute, 1978), p. 53.

4. Simonton, *Getting Well Again*, p. 41.

5. Halpern, *Tuning the Human Instrument*, p. 49.

6. Bloomfield, *The Holistic Way to Health and Happiness*, p. 50.

13. DEATH, DYING, AND REIKI

1. Jacobi, *C. G. Jung: Psychological Reflections*, p. 28.

2. Croissant, *Continuum—the Immortality Principle*, p. 7.

3. Ibid., p. 1.

4. Ibid., p. 21.

5. Ibid., p. 23.

6. Ibid., p. 35.

7. Ibid.

8. Ibid., p. 71.

9. Elisabeth Kubler-Ross, *Death—the Final Stage of Growth* (Englewood Cliffs: Prentice-Hall, Inc., 1975), p. 6.

14. INSTANTANEOUS HEALING WITH REIKI

1. Quoted by Ferguson in *The Aquarian Conspiracy*, p. 174.

2. Morris (ed.), *The American Heritage Dictionary of the English Language*, p. 680.

3. Ibid., p. 1248.

Selected Bibliography

Barnett, Lincoln. *The Universe and Dr. Einstein.* New York: Bantam Books, 1969.

Beasley, Victor. *Your Electro-Vibratory Body.* Boulder Creek, Calif.: University of the Trees Press, 1978.

Bloomfield, Harold, and Kory, Robert. *The Holistic Way to Health and Happiness.* New York: Simon & Schuster, 1978.

Brenner, Paul. *Health Is a Question of Balance.* New York: Vantage Press, 1978.

Capra, Fritjof. *The Tao of Physics.* New York: Bantam Books, 1977.

Dossey, Larry. *Space, Time & Medicine.* Boulder: Shambhala Publications, Inc., 1982.

Ferguson, Marilyn. *The Aquarian Conspiracy.* Los Angeles: J. P. Tarcher, 1980.

Hall, Manly. *Freemasonry of the Ancient Egyptians.* Los Angeles: Philosophical Research Society, Inc., 1980.

Halpern, Steven. *Tuning the Human Instrument.* Belmont, Calif.: Spectrum Research Institute, 1978.

Kaslof, Leslie. *Wholistic Dimensions in Healing: A Resource Guide.* New York: Doubleday & Co., Inc., 1978.

Keyes, Ken. *Handbook to Higher Consciousness.* St. Mary, Kentucky: Living Love Publications, 1975.

Kübler-Ross, Elisabeth. *On Death and Dying.* New York: Macmillan Publishing Co., Inc., 1970.

————. *Death—The Final Stage of Growth.* Englewood Cliffs: Prentice-Hall, Inc., 1975.

Montagu, Ashley. *Growing Young.* New York: McGraw-Hill, 1981.

Motoyama, Hiroshi. *Science and the Evolution of Consciousness.* Brookline, Mass.: Autumn Press, Inc., 1978.

Ott, John. *Health and Light.* New York: Pocket Books, 1976.

Sagan, Carl. *Cosmos.* New York: Random House, 1980.

Selye, Hans. *Stress without Distress.* New York: Signet, 1975.

Sheehy, Gail. *Pathfinders.* New York: William Morrow and Co., Inc., 1981.

Simonton, Carl and Simonton, Stephanie. *Getting Well Again.* New York: Bantam Books, 1978.

Swami Rama. *A Practical Guide to Holistic Health.* Honesdale, Penn.: Himalayan International Institute, 1978.

Teilhard de Chardin, Pierre. *Toward the Future.* Translated by Rene Hague. New York: William Collins Sons & Co. Ltd., and Harcourt Brace Jovanovich, Inc., 1975.

Talbot, Michael. *Mysticism and the New Physics.* New York: Bantam Books, 1981.

Wolf, Fred. *Taking the Quantum Leap.* New York: Harper & Row, 1981.

Zukav, Gary. *The Dancing Weu Li Masters: An Overview of the New Physics.* New York: Bantam Books, 1980.

I especially appreciate Dr. Ray for her continued help and service to us during John's final time on this earth. Her dedication to the Reiki and to sharing it with us and with all humankind is reflected in her teachings and in *The Reiki Factor.*

ELIZABETH VALERIUS WARKENTIN, PH.D.

January 1985

Psychotherapist and Adjunct Professor of Psychology,
Georgia State University
Reiki Master/Teacher, Atlanta, Georgia

Preface

This book is a landmark. It is the first book published about Reiki! The word "Reiki" means universal life-force energy. Reiki is a wonderful, unique, profound, and safe technique for activating and amplifying the natural life-force energy within you and for applying this energy to yourself using a precise and scientific method.

Reiki is a powerful yet gentle, subtle yet precise art and science of restoring your depleted energy and of balancing natural energy within you to promote healing, positive wellness, wholeness, higher consciousness, and, ultimately, enlightenment.

Reiki is not a religion, it is not a dogma, it is not a doctrine, and it is not a cult. Reiki is not a "laying-on-of-hands"—a term that is used in a religious context and is a form of healing involving a strong degree of belief in a particular religion. Reiki is not a belief system nor is it a form of mind control, hypnosis, or wishful thinking.

What, then, is Reiki? It is a natural energy-activating method. It is a precise way of using "light-energy" to restore and balance your own vital energy—physically, emotionally, and mentally—and to connect with your inner self—your spirit. This book puts you in touch with the essence of Reiki. This book is also about Reiki, which means that it contains descriptions. It cannot contain the experience itself. By clearly and directly getting to what the essence of Reiki is and by including discussions of many people's experiences with Reiki, I have hoped to facilitate your understanding of it.

Reiki is easy to learn, completely safe, and requires no

special knowledge or additional equipment. You can learn to
use Reiki in almost any situation or location, at any time of
day that is suitable for your own personal needs. There is no
need to alter your consciousness while you are using Reiki.
Reiki can be applied effectively on a daily basis to such ailments
as headaches, eyestrain, physical tensions, and fatigue, as well as
to emotional-mental responses such as anxiety, depression, fear,
uptightness, and anger. Reiki can also be used to heal and whole
chronic ailments and as a life-force support system in terminal
situations. And, for those moving in that direction, Reiki is a
precise, subtle tool for personal transformation, higher consciousness, and enlightenment.

Reiki, however, is not used just for when you are sick.
It is one of the best ways available for restoring your vital
energy, for maintaining your positive wellness, and for preventing
disorders. "Positive wellness" refers to a state of health, well-
being, and wholeness that is not simply the lack of symptoms
but reflects a high level of vitality, which is naturally your
birthright.

Who can learn Reiki? Virtually anyone of any age is capable
of learning this precise, natural, energy-balancing technique. The
basic requirement is that you have to be ALIVE on this plane
of existence. I have taught Reiki successfully to people from ages
five to ninety-three. I have taught Reiki to those who were healthy
and to those who were in varying degrees of ill health, including
those in terminal stages. I have also taught Reiki to blind people
and to those with severe physical, emotional, and mental defi-
ciencies.

Who needs Reiki? *You* do—if you are alive and using energy
in any way each day. Reiki is for the sick and tired who are
sick and tired of being sick and tired! And Reiki is for all of
you who are healthy and whole and plan to stay that way—
no matter what your age!

I have titled this book *The Reiki Factor* to reflect the deep
significance to each of us in our lives of the rediscovery and
availability now of this wonderful, profound, ancient technique

XIX

for activating the light-energy within us and for restoring and balancing our vital energy. Many who have attended my lectures and the Reiki Seminars have asked, "Is there a book about Reiki?" and "When are you going to write about Reiki?" No, until this time there was no book about Reiki. Now there is.

The primary purpose of the book is to discuss Reiki, to make it known to you, and to demonstrate the uses and benefits of Reiki in your daily life. A secondary purpose is to put Reiki in the modern context of the "so-called" New Age into which we are now evolving and to relate it to what is called a "wholistic model."

The book is designed so that you may read the chapters in any order you wish, skipping around to those of special interest to you, or read in a linear manner from beginning to end. But to assure yourself a full comprehension and deeper understanding of Reiki, please read the whole book.

Many who have already taken the Reiki seminars have called it the "gift of the universe" and "the precious gift of life." Again and again I am told, "Reiki is the best investment I have ever made in my *life*," and "I don't know how anyone lives without Reiki!"

In the end, Reiki is not words, it is not an intellectual debate, and it is not an emotional panacea. Reiki is a unique, individual *experienc*e of using natural energy in a specific way to promote balanced energy, healing, wholeness, and positive wellness in your being and in your life no matter who you are, where you are, or what your age. When Reiki is used *as instructed* on a regular basis in your life, you will be participating consciously and directly in the process of restoring your vital energy, of healing, of gaining wholeness, and of promoting higher consciousness and enlightenment of yourself according to *your own natural process*.

It is an honor to share Reiki with each of you in the form of this book. It is a privilege to have the opportunity to give public lectures and to instruct you in this incredibly gentle art and precise science of Reiki. I invite each of you to read the book, to take a Reiki Seminar, and to open the Reiki experience directly to yourself. Meanwhile, enjoy the book, learn, grow, and be well.

BARBARA RAY

Atlanta, Georgia
January 1982

Acknowledgments

There are no words adequate to express my deep gratitude for *all* who have supported and contributed time and effort to the Reiki Center in Atlanta, Georgia, and to the founding and success of the American-International Reiki Association, Inc.

Special thanks are given to the hundreds of persons who have given accounts of the profound benefits they have received from using the technique of Reiki. They will recognize their contributions throughout this book.

For his support of Reiki, of my work in wholistic health, and the A.I.R.A. certification program for Reiki teachers, many thanks go to Terry S. Friedmann, M.D., director of Holistic Medical Clinic in Venice, Florida, and one of the founders of the American Holistic Medical Association.

Thanks to Fred. W. Wright, Jr., writer-journalist; and Marvette Carter, writer-teacher-counselor, for reading and commenting upon sections of the manuscript, and to Nonie Greene and my mother, Jean Brinkman, for their constant support, humor, and long hours of "rough-draft" typing of the manuscript.

A special expression of gratitude is given for the enduring support and encouragement of my dear friends, the doctors, the psychotherapists, and other health-care professionals who have endorsed Reiki, this book, and my work in healing and wholing.

Eternal gratitude is given to the late Hawayo Takata for a deep friendship and full training in Reiki and to Dr. Mikao Usui who rediscovered this profound technique.

And, last but not least, many thanks to both of my parents for giving me the opportunity to be here now working and serving in this New Age of Humanity.

PART I

The most beautiful thing we can experience is the mysterious. It is the source of all true art and science.
Albert Einstein

1

Introduction: A New Beginning

*Only that day dawns to which we are
awake.*
                                          Thoreau

Think of it! Every day of your life represents an opportunity
for a new beginning. Every breath you take is a rebirth, drawing
in a new round of air connecting you to the universal vibrations
of that particular moment. Exhaling is a letting go or a releasing
of what has now become the past, and the new breath again
keeps you in the "here now"—the eternal present.

Life is made of energy, and energy is in perpetual motion,
moving in swirling spirals. Each moment in your life is a new
part of the unfolding spiral of your own life's process. The
very essence of life is motion—nothing is status quo. Move-
ment and change are basic, natural laws of energy—of life.

The truth is that everything you do is for the first time.
Of course, you do not forget what you have already learned.
The natural flow is learning from the past, whether it was a year
ago or a moment ago, and synthesizing this knowledge into your
being. Each new breath spirals you on to a new experience.
Every minute you are different from the one before. Some people
are "awake" to this natural phenomenon. That is, some people
are consciously aware of and in tune with this natural rhythm of

3

life-force energy running through them. Everything they do is done new, is personal, and is very much alive! These people can be called "masters."

You are a "master," too—everyone is. Adaptability, flexibility, openness, acceptance, going with the natural flow, and the ability to perceive the essence of all things are all "master" qualities.

Now that you have this book about Reiki, relax, make yourself comfortable, and allow yourself to be open to new ideas. Make the reading of this book an opportunity for learning, growing, and transforming, as well as for integrating new concepts and affirming some you already had.

The first part of the book deals with the essence of Reiki. Use your mind, your emotions, and your intuitions to grasp this essence. The words are designed to elicit from within you the perception—the insight of what Reiki *in its essence* is—beyond the limits of the words.

The second part of the book describes the uses of Reiki in your daily life and the experiences many other people have had with Reiki. All of the examples contain descriptions of Reiki but, ultimately, do not contain the experience itself. That experience you have to get directly through and within yourself.

You and I can talk endlessly about swimming, but the way we get the experience of swimming is by doing it. We can discuss many aspects of apples, but the way we really know the apple is by eating it. There is no single experience of Reiki. An experience one person has with Reiki is not "right" and another person's "wrong." Their experiences are just different from each other. *All* the experiences with using Reiki give insight to how it can and does work. Reiki is life-force, universal energy. Reiki is the dance of life energy.

As I mentioned in the preface, this book is divided into two parts and can be read in any order that suits you. For example, you might be especially interested in what Reiki can do for you in helping to release negative stress or in relaxing you. You might want to read the chapter "Stress, Relaxation, and Reiki" first and then read the other chapters. Each chapter will give you insights to Reiki that will help you understand its unique process more fully. For that reason, I recommend that, ultimately, you should read the whole book.

My basic approach was to go from the general context of Reiki as a New Age tool for energy-balancing, natural healing, maintaining positive wellness, and higher consciousness to specific discussions of what Reiki is, how it works, and examples of how it can be used in your daily life.

Part I gives a context for Reiki in modern times as we move through a transitional phase into a New Age. Then some basic guidelines are given for understanding the wholistic model and Reiki, followed by complete discussions of what Reiki is, how the technique works, and its origins.

Part II tells how the Reiki technique can be used in your daily life according to *your own personal needs,* shows how the basic principle underlying Reiki can be applied to any disease or imbalance, and demonstrates that the Reiki method does not interfere or conflict with medical treatment in any way. I have included a wide variety of individual cases demonstrating the benefits of Reiki to facilitate your understanding.

Appendix A is a section of questions I have been asked about Reiki and their answers.

Appendix B sketches some of the events in my life that led me to Reiki and provided me with the expertise to identify Reiki. Teaching Reiki Seminars and extended work at the Reiki Center gave me the fullness of direct experience with Reiki.

The verb "to heal" derives from an old English root meaning "to make whole." Throughout this book, I have used the word "wholing" as synonymous with healing to convey the idea of wholeness. I have also coined the term "light-energy" in referring to the universal, life-force energy of Reiki. The Reiki activating-energy transmissions tap you directly into this high-level natural light-energy of a cosmic order. You can then use this connection in the ways that are best suited to you as a natural energy source for healing, wholing, and maintaining positive wellness and even for achieving in a natural way higher consciousness or what some call "cosmic consciousness." In modern physics, the question of consciousness has arisen in connection with quantum theory. As Robert Toben stated in *Space-Time and Beyond,* "Consciousness is the missing hidden variable in the structure of matter."

In discussing Reiki both in this book and in my public lectures and seminars, I try to convey what the essence of Reiki is and how it works with as little interpretation *as is possible* because of the limitations of words. Reiki is a technique for connecting oneself to life-force energy and for applying this energy. What you do with Reiki depends on your own individual needs as your life's process unfolds.

One of the meanings of the verb "to interpret" is "to translate." Everyone knows that in verbal interpretations, something is lost in the translation. When you describe an experience to a friend, even when you retell it in your own words, it is never quite the same as the original experience.

Interpretations tend to impose limits, putting things into square boxes rather than keeping them in the flow of naturally spiraling energy. Interpretations often include projections of your own psychological blocks and thereby alter or color what was really there. Interpretations also tend to create illusions, that is, they tend to keep you from seeing that *what is, is.*

Interpretations often keep you locked into the past with closed doors and lead you to rigid categorizing. The closest I have come to catergorizing Reiki is to call it a self-help technique, which it is.

Some people have interpreted and catergorized Reiki as simply a body therapy. That is partly true. But, as will be demonstrated throughout this book, Reiki is more than a physical treatment. Others have interpreted and categorized Reiki as occult. "Occult" is defined as "of, pertaining to, dealing with, or knowledgeable in supernatural influences, agencies or phenomena; beyond the realm of human comprehension; mysterious; inscrutable."[1] Only to the extent that life itself is mysterious is Reiki occult. Even Albert Einstein acknowledged the mystery of life in his words, "The most beautiful thing we can experience is the mysterious. It is the source of all true art and science."[2]

Through the years, I have heard many other interpretations and partial truths expressed about Reiki. Most of these interpretations simply reflect the limited perspective of the persons making them. That statement is not intended as judgment but rather as discernment.

As you continue to read, keep yourself open and absorb the material rather than interpreting it. Let the words guide you rather than block you, and let the meaning resonate and connect within you. In this way, you will discover for yourself what Reiki is. If you take the Reiki Seminar, you will have the direct, "no-words-in-between" experience of Reiki. Reiki is in its essence a freeing, liberating, healing, natural energy.

As outlined above, I have included in Appendix B some details of my journey to find Reiki and how my academic studies enabled me to recognize it for what it is. Deep within me, I had known that this ancient technique for activating from within a person a high order of universal life energy was still on this planet. I just did not know where to find it. Gradually, certain events unfolded in my life that brought me in direct contact with Reiki, transforming my life and opening all the dimensions of being that I had known were there.

2

Dawning of a New Age

*There are "events" in the human mass,
just as there are in the world of organic
matter, or in the crust of the earth, or in
the stellar universe; and so there are also
certain privileged beings who are present
at and share in such events.*
            Pierre Teilhard de Chardin

You and I are these privileged beings living together and sharing in one of the most profound moments of human evolution and history. We are living and participating in one of those "events" in the human mass to which Chardin was referring and to which has often been applied the term the "dawning of the Age of Aquarius." We seem to be in a profound transitional period, moving from what was called the Age of Pisces to that of Aquarius or from the Industrial Age to that of Technology or Space.

We are living in a time when civil unrest and political upheavals occur almost daily, when terrorists play power games with governments and with the lives of hostages, when inflation soars seemingly out of control, when the assassin's gun aims indiscriminately at political and religious leaders, when many twentieth-century Cassandras cry doom for all of us, and when

8

parents wonder what to do about a child's relationship with computerized machines.

Yet in the midst of the worldwide confusion, conflict, and chaos and the harangue of the modern chorus of prophets chanting doom, a new civilization appears to be arising. A new pattern is emerging and is visible upon the horizon, marking the birthing and ascendance of a New Age of expanded human consciousness. What makes this particular phase we are experiencing so confusing yet so provocative, so frightening yet so inspiring, is the realization that profound change and transformation are stirring many of us individually and some in groups to the awakening of a new level of human consciousness all over this planet.

Interestingly enough, the traditional symbolism for the Age of Aquarius is the water-bearer—a fully awakened person pouring water, representing knowledge, to everyone on this earth plane. Whoever drinks of the water will be transformed to a higher state of consciousness, a higher state of being. This symbolism shows clearly that the Age of Aquarius is an age when all of humanity makes a choice to grow, to change, and to transform.

The knowledge and the power to transform are available to everyone by learning to open the channel to a higher order of energy and by consciously tapping or connecting to that inner power. On another level, the knowledge and power to transform are available to many nations in the famous formula $E = MC^2$ of Albert Einstein. The choice is ours whether to use our technology, power, and energy to create wars or peace, to foster hatred or unconditional love, or to annihilate ourselves or create a new world order. The key is in our consciousness. "To be or not to be?" is still the main issue for reflection by all of us.

The good news is that this Aquarian Age will unfold through approximately the next twenty-five hundred years. I find it helpful to keep this time span in mind. When viewed from the wholistic perspective of hundreds of years, stages of this unfolding process into mankind's New Age of a higher evolution are easier to identify. The phase we are currently in is that of the birthing or what some have called the transitional phase or passage to another cycle of human life and consciousness. The transition to this New Age began during this past century, and new *light* is dawning everywhere on this planet. As Alvin Toffler so aptly and succinctly puts it in his book *The Third Wave,* "A new civilization is emerging in our lives, and blind men everywhere are trying to suppress it."[1] Then he emphatically reminds us that "the dawn of this new civilization is the single most explosive fact of our life-times."[2]

Periods of transition in human history as well as in individual lives are always characterized by conflict and confusion. The old patterns of being and the old ways of existing always resist the new patterns of becoming and the new ways of perceiving. So, too, in the current process of transformation, which is affecting our entire planet, the struggles, conflicts, despairs, and deaths are signs of the birthing of a new phase of human evolution.

The single most outstanding feature of this New Age of humanity is the awakening consciousness of mankind as a whole.

In *The Aquarian Conspiracy,* Marilyn Ferguson describes it as a "new mind—the ascendance of a startling worldview that gathers into its framework breakthrough science and insights from earliest recorded thought." As will be demonstrated throughout this book, Reiki is a technique rediscovered from man's past, and it is thousands of years old. Reiki is a connection with light-energy that includes a precise, self-help, transformative technique which is both an art and a science that can be easily and safely learned by nearly anyone. In Chapter 8, the re-emergence of Reiki as a New Age tool is traced.

Expanding consciousness means going beyond the old limits and extending to a larger sphere. By analogy, to comprehend that the world encompasses more than the home, a child might be given a model of home, street, city, and state. As the child begins to understand a perspective bigger than his home, he can then be given an expanded model of state, plus many states, plus United States (country), plus other countries, and including the concept of "world" or "planet." To hold onto only the model of "home" would be to limit severely our human capacity for conceptual growth. To include the understandings gained from the model of "home" but also to expand to the consciousness of "world" and ultimately to "universe" or "cosmos" would be to experience our innate capacity for continuous, unlimited expansion of consciousness.

For nearly two hundred years, Isaac Newton's model of mechanical clockwork universe dominated modern physics. Newtonian law was essentially one of cause and effect, as demonstrated by billiard balls hitting one another and moving in a predictable pattern of response. The Newtonian perspective tended to be linear and mechanistic. But as scientific investigation continued, based for the most part on Newton's model, an increasing amount of data did not fit into that framework.

Early in this century, Einstein's special theory of relativity presented a new, expanded paradigm for comprehending the universe. The old model was not entirely wrong, but the new one offered by Einstein went beyond the limits set by Newton and forced a more inclusive, wholistic view. The new model that emerged has enabled scientists to gain an enormously increased comprehension of the universe. The transformations in our lives triggered by new physics reminds me of Dorothy's remark in the *Wizard of Oz,* "Goodness, Toto, I've a feeling we're not in Kansas anymore!" Likewise, these new perspectives have transformed our daily lives in a myriad of ways through technological advances applied from our kitchens to our offices and from our bodies to our spirits! I have a feeling we are not in the past anymore!

A new paradigm by its larger perspective transforms old knowledge and unveils new dimensions for our exploration and experience. Manifesting in the dynamics of this New Age of expanding consciousness is the paradigmatic change from a mechanistic to a wholistic perspective. It is true, of course, that throughout human history certain individuals and even small, specialized groups have exhibited a "wholistic consciousness." The good news of today's world is that everywhere on this planet millions of people from all social, economic, professional, and educational levels are awake or are in the process of awakening to this model—this vision of wholeness.

Indeed, the evolutionary process of this New Age of humanity has already begun, and the ancient technique of Reiki has re-emerged as a transformative tool for energy balancing, for natural healing, for wholing, and for creating peace, joy, love, and, ultimately, for achieving higher consciousness and enlightenment.

3

The Wholistic Model

The shift from the mechanistic to the holistic conception of reality is likely to result in a transformation of unprecedented dimension.

Fritjof Capra

The word "holistic," sometimes spelled with a *w* as wholistic, derives from the Greek word *holos* meaning to view something from the functional interrelationship of all its parts. In essence, the wholistic paradigm offers a dynamic model of seeing and considering everything as an organic whole. The dictionary definition of "whole" includes the concepts of "containing all component parts, not disjoined but unified and restored, healthy and *healed*."

In skillfully applying principles of wholeness in your daily life, you will begin to develop a perspective that increases your inner sensitivity to your entire being—physically, emotionally, mentally, and spiritually. Likewise, through the process of shifting your model to one of wholeness, you will be able to see yourself with clarity in your external relationships with other people and with your environment. In shifting to a wholistic model, you will be expanding to a consciousness that will affect profoundly your entire living process. You will be opening yourself

to vast insights and to a new sense of confidence in the unfolding of your life process.

The wholistic perspective shifts your vision to be inclusive
rather than exclusive; it expands rather than restricts; it is
spherical rather than square; and it allows you to see the whole
pattern, putting the pieces into perspective relative to each other
rather than as isolated, unconnected parts.

On paper, the wholistic model is a circle or a mandala that
appears static, flat, and two-dimensional. In reality and in consciousness, this model is in motion like the counterclockwise,
spiraling energy of a spiral galaxy. Life is motion. Life is multi-
dimensional.

With the wholistic model, you are able to see and to intuit the
interconnectedness of all things. You can see the natural flow
of energy. From ancient to modern times, Eastern mystics have
spoken of the essential unity and interrelatedness of all natural
phenomena. All things were seen as a manifestation of basic
oneness and as a part of a greater, cosmic whole. Twentieth-
century physics now reveals that this wholeness appears to be a
universal reality. In *The Tao of Physics* Fritjof Capra states that
the study of subatomic particles has revealed "the same insight—
that the constituents of matter and the basic phenomena involving
them are all interconnected, interrelated and interdependent; that
they cannot be understood as isolated entities, but only as
integrated parts of the whole."

In the personal search for self, the journey often begins
with outer forms and tends to move to inner levels of experience
and knowledge. So we will begin with the concepts of wholistic
health and keep in mind that these principles apply to the physical
dimension of our being as well as to the emotional, mental, and
spiritual aspects of ourselves.

The concept of wholistic health and living can best be expressed in the statements, "the whole is greater than the sum
of its parts" and "a house is more than a collection of bricks."
The wholistic approach to your life means looking at all of the
parts together as well as that which sustains the harmony among
the parts. "That which sustains the harmony" is the dimension I

will refer to throughout this book as "spiritual." The implication, wholistically speaking, is that in addition to our physical, emotional, or mental experiences, life consists of an essence called the "spiritual dimension," and everyone has it!

In using the wholistic principles in reference to your health, you will be shifting your paradigm, that is, your model, from a mechanistic (monistic) to a wholistic one. The mechanistic view of health that has literally dominated modern Western medicine viewed the body as a machine with parts that are to be treated separately. The emphasis is on the physical body with little or no attention to the emotional, mental, and spiritual dimensions of ourselves. The mechanistic approach is not wrong in that it recognizes a need to treat an injured or diseased physical part; but it tends to exclude the greater truth that *all* parts of your being must be activated in the healing process or in the process of maintaining positive wellness and wholeness.

In contrast, the wholistic approach takes into account as many aspects of the individual as possible. For purposes of illustration, let us assume that as a child you fell while playing at school. The physical injury you received was as minor as a bruise or a scratch. You were treated for the physical injury and sent back to class. Now imagine that while falling you were feeling not only the physical pain but you were also having the emotional response of embarrassment, inferiority, and shame when your classmates laughed at your fall. Add to this your mental response of wishing you were not there or perhaps thinking you had done something wrong and were being punished by God. Now imagine that many years have passed and as an adult you are faced with a difficult injury or disease. Your conscious mind has long forgotten the little episode at school, but your present physical plight elicits the old feelings of embarrassment, inferiority, and shame. You spend a great deal of time wishing you did not have the condition, and you feel punished by God or possibly even denying such a force as Divine intelligence in the cosmos!

In approaching this situation from a wholistic perspective, all of the above-mentioned responses would be taken into consideration. Not only would the physical injury or disease be treated with a variety of physical therapies, but, in addition, therapies for the emotional, mental, and spiritual bodies would be explored. To quote a well-known phrase, "A house is more than a collection of bricks." You, indeed, are more than a collection of bones, veins, and organs!

The mechanistic approach tends to treat symptoms, whereas the wholistic approach looks for recurrent patterns. Symptoms and causes are examined and treated, and the individual involved has an opportunity for growth on many levels of being. Manifestations of disease, pain, and other signals of distress are regarded as important information about conflicts, imbalances in energy use, and disharmony of elements within the person. Disease on any level of your being is viewed as a process for expanding your consciousness by increasing your sensitivity to the interrelated energy fields of the body-emotion-mind-spirit dynamic. In the wholistic model, the primary concern is with the integrated, whole person. To settle for less in your life is to limit your innate potential for growth and to deny your birthright to health, wholeness, and enlightenment.

In the mechanistic model of healing, emphasis is placed primarily on the ability of someone else to heal you. You were perhaps taught from early childhood, whenever you were ill, broken down, or in some way not physically whole, to give someone else the responsibility for making you well or for "fixing" you. The primary message you received was to go to the outside for healing and surrender to someone else *your power* for restoring your own health. In that process, you could easily experience a sense of loss of your own "life power," resulting in feelings of helplessness, depression, and defeat. You could grow to resent the physician who is attempting to help you if healing results are not forthcoming as expected or additional complications arise. In such a state, you can begin to feel that you are worthless and powerless and have no control whatever over your own life process.

Again, the mechanistic approach is not wrong in its assumption that other people possibly can help you. Its perspective, however, is not large enough. In contrast, the wholistic model has as one of its basic tenets the concept that *you* assume responsibility for your healing process and maintenance of health. The assumption is that as a living, active individual, you *do* have certain significant and fundamental controls over your life, that you *can* make intelligent choices for yourself, and that you *do* have the power, within you, to restore and maintain your health. The wholistic model shifts the responsibility of wellness to the individual and thereby presents the opportunity for you to realize that in the most essential ways *you are in charge of your life!* In shifting your personal consciousness to a wholistic model, you would not necessarily eliminate seeking assistance and guidance from others. But the relationships between you and the other persons would be one of interaction, support, and interrelating rather than one of dependency, powerlessness, and hopelessness.

In addition, it is important to note that in the traditional mechanistic approach treatment generally begins when a disease has manifested tangibly but that little or no attention is given to preventive techniques or to the development of a science of wholeness. In going to a larger perspective, the wholistic approach deals not only with the manifested disease but also emphasizes preventive techniques and encourages you as an individual to develop an approach to positive wellness and wholeness that is best suited to your particular needs, preferences, and lifestyle. A leading exponent of wholistic medicine, Dr. Harold Bloomfield maintains, "It may be convincingly argued that modern medicine has achieved unprecedented success in treating disease but has proven virtually incapable of promoting health."[1]

In shifting from the mechanistic to the wholistic model, you will need to select tools that are inherently designed to expand consciousness on all levels of your being—techniques that activate and promote integration of the body-emotion-mind-spirit dynamic. As Marilyn Ferguson appropriately states, "The difference between transformation by accident and transformation by a system is like the difference between lightning and a

lamp. Both give illumination, but one is dangerous and un-
reliable, while the other is relatively safe, directed, available."[2]
Reiki, in and of itself, is a complete, safe system for personal
healing, wholing, and transforming which simultaneously includes
your body-emotion-mind-spirit dynamic. In its essence, Reiki is
a contact with natural energy—it is a way of activating and
amplifying the power within you. As a natural, energy-balancing
method, Reiki is safe and easy to use.

Reiki also is a special technique for directing natural energy
in such a way that your entire being is transformed and illumi-
nated *according to the process which is uniquely and naturally
yours.* Unlike many other techniques and therapies, Reiki can
be used effectively in combination with other methods for
healing and transformation. In expanding to a wholistic approach to your health and life, Reiki provides a direct method
for activating your inner power. With Reiki, you can naturally
accept responsibility for your own health and well-being. Reiki
also helps minimize your sense of helplessness and powerlessness
when faced with physical, emotional, mental, or spiritual
struggles and imbalances. In addition, when used as instructed,
Reiki provides you with an essential preventive technique and a
means of developing positive wellness and wholeness maintenance
regardless of your age.

In summary, it can be seen in answering the question, "What
is wholistic health and living?" the wholistic model offers an
approach to living that emphasizes the importance of integrating
into every aspect of your life process all levels of your being—
physical, emotional, mental, and spiritual. In applying this
wholistic model to health, healing, and everyday living, all
dimensions of your self are taken into account as important
even though different in nature. The wholistic perspective gives
you an awareness of yourself as "uniquely *you*" as well as a
sensitivity to a larger vision of yourself in relation to others as
you journey through your life's unfolding process.

Your expanding consciousness will also allow you to become
sensitive in a new way to your oneness with all people. You
will gain a deeper appreciation of the wonderful diversity in

manifested life forms. By living your life from a perspective of wholeness you will each day be celebrating the realization of a new consciousness of our basic unity within our diversity.

The self-help technique of Reiki is a unique way of getting in touch with the life-force energy and of promoting your own healing and wholing, of maintaining positive wellness, and of naturally opening yourself to a higher consciousness. Reiki can easily, safely, and effectively be combined with whatever other therapies or tools you are using on a daily basis.

4

What Is Reiki?

Reiki is Wisdom and Truth.
Hawayo Takata

Modern scientists have analyzed the world with an amazing degree of sophistication. The material world has been divided into finer and finer particles only to discover that deep inside the tunnel, at the ultimate center of "what is," we find energy. We have discovered the simple truth that energy precedes matter just as emotions and thoughts precede action.

More than forty-five hundred years ago, the Chinese postulated that a subtle system of life-sustaining energy circulates living physical bodies. This energy is called "ki" and is pronounced "key." *Ki* is the basic life-force energy or *vital energy* found in all living things and has just that meaning as the suffix on the word, Reiki.

Basic to all Oriental healing arts is the concept that *ki* is the vital life force upon which physical life is dependent. In Chinese *ki* is *Chi,* in Hindu it is *prana,* and in English breath and ectoplasm come closest to the essential meaning of *ki.* Russian researchers call it *bioplasmic* energy, Hippocrates called it *nature's life force,* the Kahunas called it *mana,* and Christ called it *light.* It has also been called *cosmic energy, bioenergy,* and *vital force.* The harmony, amount, and balance of this vital energy of *ki* within you is essential for the health and the proper functioning of your being in this life. *Ki* energy is finer than electricity but is related to it.

The state of *ki* in your system relates to the body-mind harmony or disharmony you are experiencing in your daily life. Indeed, the balance, amount, and quality of your *ki* is influenced by a variety of aspects such as air quality, food, amounts and kinds of stress, heredity factors, and environmental conditions. To maintain a balance in your health physically, emotionally, mentally, and spiritually, you need an unpolluted source to restore your vital energy *(ki)*.

At your birth, you have a certain level of *ki*, vital energy. As you live each day, you tend to expend varying amounts of energy. Therefore, each day you need natural sources for replenishing your energy expenditures. When you continue to expend more energy than you restore on all levels of your being, you often are faced with physical, emotional, and mental imbalances or diseases. With low or drained vital energy, you are inclined toward physical fatigue and illness as well as emotional and mental exhaustion. You can become irritable, angry, hostile, and even paranoid. You can have difficulty thinking clearly, and you can be constantly tired, exhausted, and even depressed. Indeed, in such depleted states, it is difficult for you to feel spiritually uplifted and inspired.

Reiki (pronounced "ray-key") is an Oriental word meaning "universal life energy." The term "Reiki" has been applied to a specific technique for restoring and balancing your natural life-force energy. Reiki is neither a dogma nor a religion but is a complete, scientific method for self-healing and for maintaining your health and sense of well-being physically, emotionally, mentally, and spiritually. Reiki is an effective technique for prevention of diseases and energy imbalances on all levels of your being. Reiki is also a unique, highly effective tool for personal transformation, growth, and change. Reiki is a natural energy-balancing and renewing method that can be used in conjunction with any other technique of health-care treatment as well as with any other personal growth therapy. Reiki does not conflict with traditional medicine but can be used with it or as an additional source for restoring vital energy and promoting health and well-being.

The Reiki method of natural healing is designed to strengthen systematically your absorption of vital life energy. When tensions develop in your physical body or blocks occur in your mind or emotions, your flow of vital energy can stagnate and be depleted excessively. You begin, then, to break down physically and emotionally. You see things as if in a fog and sometimes feel as though you will never recover. The constant stress and daily pressures typical of modern life often result in our being increasingly alienated from natural healing energies.

By using the Reiki technique in your daily life, you will gradually be able to regain your energy balance. Once you have accumulated enough *ki* for your normal maintenance and functioning, you will be able to reserve and conserve energy. The Reiki method puts energy into your body in a specific manner. Reiki regulates and balances the *ki* flow as needed specifically by *your* body. By balancing and restoring your vital energy, *ki*, you will be working directly with natural energy.

The special technique of Reiki puts you in direct contact with natural energy and in touch with the flow of *ki* in your being. In using Reiki, you will be working to heal the causes of diseases, imbalances, and disorders rather than merely treating symptoms. Symptoms are important signals that something is off balance and that you are losing energy without sufficient renewal. For healing to occur, however, the cause of the symptom must be treated or released. Therefore, in using the Reiki technique you may also need to work with the outer and inner conditions that influence your *ki* state.

The Reiki technique helps you to regain balance physically, emotionally, mentally, and spiritually. The use of Reiki will involve you directly with your own healing and daily renewing process. If you are not actually experiencing an illness, you will be restoring and balancing energy that you have depleted in the course of your normal, daily activities. Reiki is one of the most efficient relaxation and stress-reduction techniques available to modern man. Reiki has the additional benefits of requiring no special conditions or equipment except *yourself* and a seminar of instruction in Reiki by a certified Reiki Master/ Teacher. Once you have learned this technique, Reiki can be used throughout the day in a variety of locations and situations. Reiki, indeed, is as natural as breathing.

5

The Technique of Reiki

Health is no more than a question of balance.

Paul Brenner, M.D.

The actual technique of the Reiki method of natural healing and energy balancing can be taught to anyone by a certified Reiki Master/Teacher. The term "Reiki Master" traditionally refers to one who has mastered this art of natural healing and is capable of teaching this method to another person.

Reiki is a simple and direct technique which I have taught successfully to people from ages five to ninety-three. I have taught Reiki to healthy people interested in preventive methods, relaxation, stress release, and restoring natural energy. I have also taught Reiki to people with diseases ranging from simple colds to terminal cancer. If an individual is partially or totally incapacitated, family members, friends, and therapists are encouraged to take the Reiki Seminar to learn how to give the Reiki treatment. In the workshop, people learn not only to use Reiki on themselves but also to apply the technique to family members or friends when needed.

It is not unusual for entire families to take the Reiki Seminar since it is a technique that can be shared easily. Even young children can be taught to give a Reiki treatment to themselves

24

and other family members. Sharing a Reiki session with family members or friends gives a beautiful opportunity for being together in a warm, caring, and peaceful atmosphere. Many people have written to share with me that Reiki has become an important element in their family life and has been a primary factor in increasing understanding of one another. One woman from Illinois wrote, "Reiki has been such a meaningful addition to our family life that we don't know what we would do without it."

Reiki is a scientific methodology. It has a precise system which you can continue to use throughout your entire life. You are able to experience the results and to identify objectively the benefits of Reiki on a personal level by following the simple steps and by checking your progress over an adequate period of time. All scientific methods are repeatable and by definition, give knowledge gained through experience. So it is with the Reiki technique.

The Reiki technique applies natural vital energy in a systematic treatment to your body. In brief, the treatment begins at the top of the head and in four steps covers the eyes, the sinus tracts, the brain, the pituitary and pineal glands, the throat, and the thyroid gland. In this step, all anatomy from the neck up is treated. In the next four steps, the lungs, heart, liver, gallbladder, stomach, spleen, pancreas, intestines, bladder, and reproductive organs are treated thoroughly. There are four steps for covering your back, which include the heart, lungs, adrenal glands, kidneys, spinal cord, lower back, and intestines. In the Reiki Seminar, complete details are given regarding this treatment and the use of Reiki with specific diseases and/or as a health and wholeness maintenance technique.

In these twelve steps, all of your major organs, glands, and veins are treated with natural energy. It is difficult even for modern medicine to determine the cause of many diseases and imbalances. Therefore, by treating the entire body with Reiki, you will be helping to heal the causes of disease and imbalances as well as eliminating the effect or symptoms. Treating the symptom is not enough. The key to complete healing—wholing and transformation—is in healing or wholing the cause. In addition, you will learn in the Reiki Seminar to treat other body parts. You will learn a Reiki technique for treating heart attacks, emphysema, varicose veins, hemorrhoids, prostate problems, hiccups, nosebleeds, accidents, and emotional and mental problems.

Embodied in the scientific method of the actual Reiki treatment is a complete art of balancing and aligning the seven major *chakras* or subtle *centers* of energy, which are located from the base of the spine to the top of the head. When you begin your Reiki treatment at the top of your head or at your crown center and work downward to the base of the spine, you will be *simultaneously* restoring and balancing natural energy in your physical body as well as in these more subtle energy centers. In the Reiki Seminar, once you are given the activating energy transmissions and are taught the Reiki method, you receive basic information about human physiology as well as the nature of these subtle energy centers. There is a direct relationship between certain glands in the endocrine system, the subtle energy chakra-centers, and your emotional-mental and spiritual balance.

The Reiki method in its specific treatment automatically both restores depleted energy in these centers and promotes balancing, healing, or wholing throughout all levels of your being. Certain positions in the Reiki technique are for specific use when you are undergoing emotional or mental distress. This technique can be used virtually any place you are as well as in any situation. The Reiki technique is simple, direct, safe, and easy to learn. The actual activating energy transmissions included in the Reiki Seminar are completely harmless and, indeed, are a unique, special experience for each individual. Once you have received the Reiki activating energy transmission you will be able to tap natural, life-force energy for the rest of your life—it cannot wear out, fall apart, or become obsolete! In fact, the more you use the Reiki, the more abundantly the energy will flow.

Reiki treats the body as a *whole* and naturally aligns energy in the body-emotions-mind-spirit dynamic. Reiki restores vital energy to all the interrelated parts of your being and promotes your natural, inner tendency to grow in the direction of health and wholeness. Each of us has a vast untapped source for vitality, fulfillment, creativity, wholeness, and consciousness which can be extended far beyond the degree experienced by most people. Positive wellness and wholeness is our Divine birthright. With Reiki, you can tap the source directly and claim the wholeness that is rightfully and naturally yours!

Included in the Reiki Seminar is a series of four activating energy transmissions to each individual participant. The Reiki Master/Teacher has mastered a process for activating energy within you. The teacher is not using personal energy in this activating process but, on another level, is tapping universal life energy. The transfers require no special knowledge on the part of the participant but do enable the individual learning the Reiki technique to channel and direct life-force energy in a precise way.

One of the best analogies I know of for describing the phenomenon of the Reiki activating energy transmissions is that of turning on a switch. Once it is done the energy begins to flow. You are the channel through which the universal life energy flows unimpeded. The more you use it the more abundant is this energy flow. The supply cannot run out because the source is unlimited. You cannot drain yourself of energy because you are acting as a channel *through* which the energy is flowing. The flow of the light-energy of Reiki is like a current of electricity that needs to be "plugged-in" and "switched-on" before a certain level of current will flow. You are then able to direct this flow of light-energy in any number of ways to meet your specific needs and circumstances.

THE DEGREES OF REIKI

Reiki is a complete method for activating and learning to use natural energy to promote healing, wholing, personal growth, transformation, and even enlightenment. The Reiki method has been kept intact in its essence as it has been preserved and transmitted through the centuries. It is composed of three main levels or degrees. The person taking First Degree Reiki can stop at that point or could continue on through the series to what is best suited to his needs. The choice to go on into the deeper levels is, of course, an individual one. An analogy to these three degrees of Reiki can be made to three degrees from a university. The First Degree of Reiki is analogous to the B.A., which gives the student a firm basis of knowledge that can then be used with success throughout his or her life. The M.A. degree takes the student deeper into specific areas, and the Ph.D. is another dimension entirely beyond the previous two degrees. Similarly, the Second and Third degrees delve more deeply into the Reiki technique.

First Degree Reiki

First Degree Reiki is the basic course in Reiki, which includes four separate energy-activating transmissions per person and complete training in the scientific use of the Reiki technique. You are taught how to give the Reiki treatment to yourself and then how to give it to family members. In the Reiki Seminar, you learn about principles of wholistic health and living, receive guidelines to positive wellness, and participate in a detailed discussion of how to benefit from Reiki in treating specific diseases as well as how to use it as a preventive method and a transformative technique.

Second Degree Reiki

The Second Degree of Reiki is available to anyone who has already completed the First Degree. It is usually suggested that a person wait at least three months before advancing to this level unless personal circumstances indicate otherwise. Second Degree Reiki is comprised of:

1. A highly effective absentee-healing technique.
2. A special technique for dealing with deep-seated emotional and mental problems, which can be used when

doing the physical treatment or along with the absentee-healing method.
3. A technique for your own personal further development in achieving your desired level of wholeness.
4. A special activating energy transmission.

The purpose of the Second Degree of Reiki is to give the individual a specific technique for learning to use and to direct energy on dimensions other than the physical plane. Part of this technique is analogous to learning to send light-energy to a specific receiver in much the same way that radio or television signals are transmitted.

Third Degree Reiki

The Third Degree of Reiki is called, traditionally, the Master level. At this level of Reiki, the person is ready to learn the intricate process of doing the activating energy transmissions. The particular process of doing these energy activations or contacts has been preserved in a formula for tapping a higher order of light-energy. This level of Reiki also includes another activating energy transmission for the Master/Teacher.

In order to make available the power and radiance of the Third Degree level on a wider basis and without restricting its use to only the Teacher level, the Third Degree has been divided into two distinct phases.

The Third Degree (3A) for personal growth, transformation, increased enlightenment and serving humanity from a universal framework is now available to anyone who has completed the First and Second Degrees. This particular level of study is especially designed for those who desire to continue further into the study of Reiki without being restricted to the qualifications required for The Official Reiki Teacher Certification Program.[SM]

The Third Degree Reiki: Teacher Certification Program (3B) is the Master/Teacher level of Reiki which includes a qualifying process, and a full, professional training program reflecting high standards of excellence. When completed, the certifying program insures that the instructors have complete training in the process of doing the authentic First and Second Degree Reiki activations and have met standards for teaching an official Reiki Seminar. For additional information about The Teacher Certification Program,[SM] please write to The American-International Reiki Association in St. Petersburg, FL, see Appendix A.

To administer the authentic activating energy attunement at the Third Degree level, the person giving this attunement must have the complete knowledge of that particular process just as the correct knowledge is needed for the teacher to complete the attunement process at the First and/or Second Degree levels. In late 1979, I received complete instructions on all of the Seven Degrees of Reiki and all of the seven levels of attunements which comprise the authentic Usui System from Hawayo Takata, the only person in the Western world possessing that knowledge. Since I am the only person to whom Mrs. Takata ever entrusted this unique system in its entirety, I have the responsibility of preserving it intact and of insuring its integrity and fullness of pure, radiant power, undiluted and unpolluted.

During these past years, as the number of students studying and using the Third Degree level of Reiki has increased and as the benefits of this level continue to be discovered, the need to make available the Fourth Degree Reiki is developing naturally and organically. The whole Reiki science of energy can only be of benefit to us on this plane of existence when it is used by us. For nearly forty years, Mrs. Takata did not choose to allow others to use and experience the universal power of the Third Degree Reiki or of any other degree beyond the Third. But, ours is a different world, a different age and a different cycle; indeed, ours is a different need. Humanity has evolved to a point of critical choice about our future world, about even our future evolution. We need all the techniques we can get which help us to attain the consciousness and wholeness to make the choice for our continued evolution on Planet Earth. The authentic Usui Reiki technique can be a beneficial factor in our journey to healing/wholing, transforming and enlightening ourselves. In this unfolding process, there seems to be no reason for withholding the possibility of studying other degrees of the Reiki beyond the Third.

6

Energy and Reiki

$$E = MC^2$$

Albert Einstein

*The recognition of the role of conscious-
ness in the processes of the physical universe is a radical departure from classical
physics.*

Michael Talbot

From the scientific community comes the information that
all things are energy and the essence of energy is *light*. At the
Second World Congress of Science and Religion (June 1981),
internationally known French physicist Jean Charon put it this
way: "Matter broken down is energy and energy examined is
transparent—is LIGHT. . . . spirit is within the field of physics
now!"[1]

From the distant past to contemporary times, religious and
metaphysical texts have referred consistently to light as the
essence of all things. Einstein's conclusion that the speed of
light is the only constant in the universe has had stunning
implications for modern scientific investigation. In nature and in
the vast universe, the basic substance of all things appears to
be energy, and energy in its essence can be described as light.

Energy manifests itself in a vast variety of forms. Those

31

things which we identify as "alive" have in them a certain quality
and quantity of life-force energy or what is commonly called
"universal life energy." For purposes of identification, energy
forms have been divided into the basic elements of earth, water,
fire, and air.

When the molecular structure of an object is tightly com-
pressed, we experience the object as a solid material such as
tables, chairs, walls, and even our physical bodies. One of the
main differences between the physical properties of a wall and of
a human body is the density factor of each one. Another way of
stating it is that the wall has more mass per unit volume than
our physical, emotional, mental and spiritual bodies.

In shifting the model to a wholistic perspective, keep in
mind the basic principle that *all things are energy*. Then learn
to identify things outside of you and within you in terms of the
basic elements of earth, water, fire, and air.

All energy in its natural pure form is neutral. That is,
energy per se is neither good nor bad, positive nor negative.
All life energy is one source in the universe even as it is
manifested in a diversity of forms. Energy in certain forms is
highly visible and in other forms is mostly invisible to us.

Solid forms around us, including physical bodies, are seen
under normal circumstances by most of us. On the other hand,
our emotional bodies, identified with the element of water, tend
to be invisible though often expressed through the outer,
physical forms. One of the basic characteristics of water is its
tendency to spread when not contained. Remember the time when
you attempted to stop water overflowing a basin and to keep
it from spreading out over the entire floor? Emotions have a
similar trait. Emotions spread out and touch yourself, other
people, and your immediate environment.

Life energy expressed through the emotional body, such as
anger, affects the physical body with increased stress on internal
organs, veins, and blood pressure as well as usually resulting in
a disharmonious countenance and imbalanced actions.

Your thoughts are related to the element of air and by their very nature are less dense or "lighter" than solid forms. Consider that every minute of every day you carry with you *all* of your thoughts. Imagine attempting to carry all of your material possessions with you every minute! Unless put in some solid form, thoughts are for the most part invisible or intangible. Energy directed through your mental body results in thoughts. The life-force energy is neutral, and thoughts by themselves are neutral unless directed at someone or something through the emotional and physical bodies.

Fire is the element associated with your spirit, and spirit is your life-force energy, your Divine spark. Life energy tends to be experienced by you as heat. When the physical body dies, the fire goes out on this plane, and the heat of life leaves the body. When a fruit or vegetable is pulled from its life source, its vital energy begins to drain.

Fire can flame your passions directed into expressions of anger or of love. The fire words given to Moses by the Burning Bush, "I am that I am," are for each one of us to be conscious of our connection to the universal life force. "I am that I am" demonstrates the continuous life force of being no matter through what outer form it passes. The statement, "The whole is greater than the sum of its parts," helps clarify the concept of the spiritual fire dimension of your being. The "real you" goes beyond any of your individual parts. Wholeness of being is not destroyed even when the outer personality breaks down or is eliminated. In reflecting on consciousness, Carl Jung wrote:

> *And yet the attainment of consciousness was the most precious fruit of the tree of knowledge, the magical weapon which gave man victory over the earth and which we hope will give him a still greater victory over himself. . . . The coming of consciousness was probably the tremendous experience of primeval times, for with it a world came into being whose existence no one had suspected before. "And God said, 'Let there be light' " is the projection of that immemorial experience of the separation of consciousness from the unconscious.*[2]

Expanded consciousness gives you a new perspective from

which to view events in your life. Many women who have undergone radical mastectomies have expressed extreme physical-
emotional-mental pain suffered at the loss of a breast. When
viewed from a limited perspective, the loss of a body part might
seem like "the end of the world." Sometimes the loss of a
breast is interpreted as a loss of feminity. But the same situation
put into a wholistic framework and perceived with an expanded
consciousness would appear in a different "light." You certainly
prefer to have all of your outer physical parts in good working
order, but when faced with other alternatives, your consciousness
would allow for a flexible, expanded response.

At some time in this life, you will lose all your body,
your emotions, and your mind and will make a transition—
a death to another state of being. Even without these outer
forms, your consciousness will allow an experience of wholeness.
Death is no longer dreaded as a fearful finality but rather is
seen as a transition and a birthing to another level of being. In
essence, the fire never goes out. The light of the universe
luminates your being with cosmic life force, which is often
called Divine intelligence! The key to immortality is consciousness—is fire—is light.

Scientific findings indicate increasing evidence that we live
in a universe of purposeful mind ever evolving toward higher
consciousness. Edward Simon, the late Yale biologist, wrote,
"Life is the center where the material and spiritual forces of the
universe seem to meet and be reconciled. Spirit is born in
life."[3]

Reiki is universal life energy. Reiki is the fire of life. Reiki
is light-energy of a higher, less dense order than that of body
emotions and mind. With Reiki, this light-energy is activated
from within you. When you use the technique of Reiki, you are
actually applying light-energy throughout your being—healing,
wholing, and transformation come as a natural part of this
process. Reiki focuses your attention on directing and mastering
the use of your life energy, and energy is *light*. Enlightenment
literally means to be filled with light and to see things in a "new
light." When you are doing the Reiki technique, you are in

fact filling yourself with light. In addition to being a natural energy-balancing, energy-restoring, healing, and wholing method, Reiki is a natural consciousness-expanding technique that will put you in touch with your real self—with your own eternal being.

In summary, by using Reiki and by expanding your awareness you will become sensitive to the "life force" running through all living forms. You will be able to realize that this life force is derived from one source while manifesting in a seemingly endless array of unique, outer forms. To experience wholeness is to experience oneness with all living things—to identify with the cosmic life force—to experience yourself as pure, white light.

Attuning yourself to the awareness that all things are energy gives you a new perspective from which to grow. With Reiki, learning to direct your life-energy flow through your physical-emotional-mental bodies brings an experience of freedom from the old limits. Touching into pure consciousness gives you the experience of Spirit—of your own immortality. Dr. Evan Walker, a well-known American physicist stated, "Consciousness may be associated with all quantum mechanical processes. Consciousness may also exist without being associated with a living system."[4]

7

Reiki: A Science of Light

The timeless in you is aware of life's timelessness.

Kahlil Gibran

Throughout this book, I have described the Reiki technique in its outer form and how as well as why it works. But Reiki involves more than its outer method. Reiki is a word meaning universal life energy. In its inner dimension, Reiki is the process of touching into this life energy, the cosmic energy from which we all derive our being.

Reiki is an ancient natural energy and healing art for activating the power within us—for touching into, as it were, our real selves—for discovering our true essence. Reiki is a transformative science and healing art that opens the door to inner knowledge—to inner light. Reiki gives the gift of insight, of creativity, of healing, and of making whole. Reiki is not words or dogma but is a touching into the energy flowing through all living things. Reiki is an experience—a process that helps you attune *consciously* to what life itself is, to become aware of the energy that is being expressed as you and to the oneness we share with all that is *alive* in the universe. Reiki is light-energy and is a technique by which you can transform your consciousness and heal yourself.

36

In describing transformation in *The Aquarian Conspiracy,* Marilyn Ferguson writes, "And we discover that *everything is process.* The solid world is a process, a dance of subatomic particles. A personality is a collection of processes. Fear is a process. A habit is a process. A tumor is a process. All of these apparently fixed phenomena are recreated every moment, and they can be changed, reordered, transformed in myriad ways."[1] The essence of Reiki is light-energy that transforms us—each according to an individual unfolding process.

As I mentioned in an earlier chapter, the long journey in our personal search for our true selves most often begins with the world of outer forms. Most of our life is spent giving attention to the outer forms of ourselves such as our body, emotions, and mind. We devote most of our attention to acquiring outer possessions, and we tend to identify ourselves with these material possessions. Somewhere in our journey, however, each of us will have some experience with our True, Inner self. From this experience, individual for each of us and relating to the particular circumstances of our personal history, a knowledge of our inner dimensions will begin to grow. Sometimes we at first reject these experiences, writing them off as a delusion or trick manufactured by the mind. What we know about the world of outer forms seems definite, sure, and comfortable— even safe. What we know about the world of inner forms seems vague, indefinite, and uneasy—even fearful.

Eventually, however, each one of us will seek the techniques that put us in touch with inner experiences and inner reality. For many people, the energy of this New Age, referred to as the Aquarian Age, has speeded up this process of seeking inner truth. As individuals gain skill in tapping their inner being, of touching into their source, the inner world will become definite, sure, and safe territory. This inner knowledge will find expression in the outer forms of our lives. Many levels of our true, inner being will be revealed to us. We will all be able to live our lives with this new knowledge gained from being in touch with the expanded dimensions of ourselves. Until a person can think and know for himself from his inner source, he cannot be an intelligent, wise, and compassionate participant in this next phase of human unfoldment extending generally through the upcoming twenty-five hundred years.

In orthodox history books, we can find the accounts of one aspect of man's history on this planet. Such texts are filled with the records of man's unending wars, intrigues, and periods of empire building followed by times of destruction and transition. But there is another kind of history of man on this planet— it is what can be termed a "history of Light."

In past ages, mankind became increasingly preoccupied with the rewards of the material world. The focus of man's attention and values was material gain; accumulated wealth with its power over others; indulgence of the personal ego at the expense of others; separatism and prejudice, most frequently in reference to race, religion, and class; and blind attachment to outer forms in and of themselves. Interspersed, however, throughout the centuries, yet given little notice in traditional history texts, there were always those beings, both male and female, who advocated the "way of Light." Certainly in cultures where materialism was the basis of the value system, these highly conscious people seemed strange, unusual, threatening, and even insane. These "bearers of the Light" simply did not fit into the prevailing level of limited awareness, often called blindness. They did not "go along with the crowd" in their thinking, in their responses, and in their values: indeed, they could see the "Light," but they were often ridiculed, punished, and even put to death for their vision—for their expanded consciousness.

Fortunately, the situation is changing now. The Aquarian Age is dawning, and with dawn comes the light. Humanity is being shaken to its roots. Value systems are being examined and revolutionized. Riots, protests, marches, and strikes have become commonplace. Everyone wants a "piece of the cake," and everyone wants to express it! In this first phase of the New Age, old forms and meaningless patterns will be broken up and, from this chaos, will come a new phase of humanity's evolution—a time for the unfolding of man's inner wisdom and a time when the majority of people will know and express man's true nature-Spirit. Spirit is light, and light is the keynote of the Aquarian Age. Not by chance did this century see the discovery of electricity. Not by chance does electricity now circle our planet, "lighting up the world." All the great world teachers and all the mystics, known and unknown, have taught the truth about your real nature that "You are the light of the world."

In the New Age, each of us has the opportunity through expanded consciousness to *know* it for ourselves and to *act* as though we know it. When you *consciously* know that you are light, you can *emit* only unconditional love, brotherhood, wholeness, radiance, and the will-to-good toward your fellow being. As humanity proceeds further into the Aquarian Age, more and more people will exhibit this consciousness. More and more people will seek to know the inner light that in reality unites us, makes us one with all else that is alive. The paradigm will shift, values will change, and the prevailing consciousness will be expanded. Mankind as a whole will have the opportunity to realize that there is a higher purpose to life than the empty, meaningless, and blind pursuit of sex, money, and power. In *The Aquarian Conspiracy,* Marilyn Ferguson wrote, "Little wonder that these shifts in awareness are experienced as awakening, liberating, unifying—transforming. Given the reward, it makes sense that millions have taken up such practices within a scant few years. . . . Their lives and environments begin to transform as their minds are transformed."[2]

As you get closer to the Light, you get more whole. As is postulated by new physics, as you would approach the speed of light, the only known constant in the universe, the more transparent you would become—you would be one with it, and you would become the eternal here now. Reiki is a science of light known for more than ten thousand years and passed through the centuries as a part of the history of Light. Not by chance has this technique reemerged at the dawning of the Aquarian Age—an age that will be characterized by science and spirit.

Reiki, in its inner form, is a contact with pure life force— a contact with light-energy. In its outer form, Reiki is a specific, scientific method of applying and directing this light-energy.

Modern science now tells us that all things are energy manifesting in different forms. Dr. Jean Charon's statement, quoted in Chapter 6, from the perspective of new physics reveals that matter when examined and broken down is energy. And when examined further, energy is transparent—is light. Religions, philosophies, and mystics have always expressed the importance of light. The statement, "You are the light of the world" is an energy statement revealing your true nature.

Now modern science is placing increased importance on light. In humanity's New Age of expanded knowledge and consciousness, light brings together the worlds of science and spirit. Einstein's famous formula $E = MC^2$ tells you that light and matter are interchangeable. Light appears to be at the heart of all things. Just before this century, the Impressionists made an entire art form of light. The mystics have always known about it and have reminded us through the centuries that we are, in truth, Light. The scientist now becomes the mystic.

With light finally becoming recognized by modern science as a major factor in our health and as a healing agent, we will be able to expand our understanding of the wellness process in terms of the very substance of which we in essence appear to be composed. Dr. John Ott, who has been studying for years the effects of lighting on our health wrote, "Yes, it became clearer after a while that there was some mysterious link between light and the mental and physical health of humans."[3] Frustrated but not discouraged from his research, Dr. Ott discovered relationships between artificial lighting and the functioning of the endocrine system, certain nervous disorders, anxiety, depression, and even cancer. Dr. Ott stated, "We have advanced our knowledge on light and cancer and on light and abnormal behavior such as depression and hyperactivity. We have learned more about the effects of combinations of drugs and light on the chemical balance of the body."[4]

From Dr. Ott's current research, it is becoming apparent that the predominance of all kinds of artificial lighting is closely related to modern illnesses, chronic fatigue, and imbalances on many levels of our being. In addition, the profound effects of colored light on us physically and psychologically have been known for centuries although not entirely understood by meta-physicians, physicians, or other scientists. Our language reveals our intuitive knowledge of the link between colors and health. Such expressions as "he was green with envy; she saw red when he fired her; the color drained from his face; I was in the pink of condition" all reflect the effect of light on our moods, reactions, and physical conditions.

Dr. Ott speculates that as our knowledge of light and its effect on our health increases, "we may find ourselves being put on a 'light diet' in the same way we go on food diets today."[5] Indeed, Reiki is a "light-diet" science that you can add to your life now. With Reiki you can "feed and refuel," as it were, your entire being with pure light-energy. In combination with ap-propriate foods, exercises, and other life-sustaining elements, Reiki gives contact with the essential ingredient—the spark, the fire, the light of life.

At the biological level, all life depends on the process of plant photosynthesis in which light-energy is converted into chemical energy. Photosynthesis, the largest natural chemical process on this planet, depends on light energy. The process of Reiki is an analogous one. Reiki is the "life-light energy," which in its pure essence is light. Light is defined as "an electromagnetic radiation, a source of illumination" and "a specific amount, supply, or emission of illumination." Reiki is a word meaning universal life energy and is a way of direct contact with the universal source of illumination. By following the simple steps of applying the actual technique of Reiki to yourself, this light-energy can be converted for use by your body, emotions, and mind. During the entire process of the Reiki treatment, you are in touch with your spirit—your Light. You are applying natural light-energy from the outside in and promoting healing and wholing.

Reiki is a direct tool for personal transformation. By daily use of Reiki, your inner experiences will bring you an expanded consciousness. With Reiki you have means of being in touch with you, yourself, and with your true source Light. By analogy to plant photosynthesis, it can be seen how Reiki can also outwardly promote healing and wholing. In your outer self of body, emotions, and mind, Reiki, which provides a contact with light-energy, promotes healing, wellness, and wholeness. For some people this process is slow; yet, for others, it is quick— even instantaneous.

Ordinary light tends to be scattered. Light in the form of a laser beam is direct and coherent and is amplified greatly in power. For example, a laser beam can carry all information transmitted by all television stations to receiving sets all over the world *at the same time.* A laser beam can be projected to the moon or projected onto the human body for precise surgery without the complications of the older medical techniques. Learning to direct proper amounts of laser beam light-energy is the key to man's successful use in the future of this new-age technique.

In a similar way, the transmissions of energy in the Reiki technique put you in touch with a kind of beam of light. The specific Reiki treatment promotes the restoring, renewing, and balancing of natural energy throughout your entire being. In addition, in performing the actual process of this treatment, you will be mastering the skill of directing energy in the outer planes in alignment with the natural flow and essence of the life-force energy. Simultaneously, you will be transmitting this light-energy to the intangible planes of yourself—to your emotional and mental bodies. In this process, you will be coming in contact with and aware of your true, inner self and of the nature of what you really are—Light. Further along in your evolving with your mastered skill, you will be able to express your real self, your Light, more effectively in and through your outer forms. This outer expression of the Light from within manifests as real love, unconditional love, brotherhood, and the spirit of goodwill among all humanity.

Reiki, then, in its essence is light-energy. The technique of applying this light-energy, called Reiki, is a science of light. In your process of integrating the information I have presented throughout this book, it is hoped that you will be able to comprehend more deeply and more clearly what Reiki and its method are. It is hoped that the analogies used to explain Reiki will evoke an intuitive understanding from within each individual reader because the words themselves are too limiting. Likewise, keep in mind that in describing the essence of Reiki, the same difficulty is encountered as stated by Einstein when he wrote in 1938, "In our endeavor to understand reality we are somewhat like a man trying to understand the mechanism of a closed watch. He sees the face and the moving hands, even hears its ticking, but he has no way of opening the case. If he is ingenious he may form some picture of a mechanism which could be responsible for all the things he observes."[6]

In ancient Tibet, perhaps more than ten thousand years ago, the knowledge of our real nature was known. Down through the centuries, the information of how to contact Light has been preserved and passed, wrapped in many outer forms, displayed or concealed in symbols, and transmitted in sound. Reiki is a rediscovery of an ancient technique and is an art and science of Light brought into focus as a tool for transformation in the evolving New Age of mankind.

As Carl Sagan reminds us in *Cosmos:*

> For we are the local embodiment of a Cosmos grown to self-awareness. We have begun to contemplate our origins: starstuff pondering the stars; organized assemblages of ten billion billion billion atoms considering the evolution of atoms; tracing the long journey by which, here at last, consciousness arose . . . our obligation to survive is owed not just to ourselves but also to that Cosmos, ancient and vast, from which we spring.[7]

8

The Origin of Reiki

As individuals and as a species we are clearly designed to acquire a great deal of knowledge, and not to remain in that voluntary state of blinkered ignorance that characterizes so many who enjoy all the opportunities in the world to enlarge their minds and increase their knowledge. Most ignorance is voluntary, and there is not health in that, only narrowness, impoverishment of spirit, and bigotry.

Ashley Montagu

In looking at the history of mankind's life and activities on this planet, most of us would be impressed by the rise and fall of various groups and nations. We would note the long lists of seemingly endless wars, oppressions, destructions, and conquests. We would no doubt be impressed also with man's need for power and control over others. We would see his prejudices, hatreds, intolerance, and murders justified by the rationalizations of the prevailing political and religious dogma.

Likewise, if we looked closely enough at our history we would discover countless numbers of individuals and groups expressing a different kind of consciousness. We would hear

44

them advocating peace, brotherhood, and unconditional love. We would notice their testimonials to another way of perceiving our world, our relationship to others, and our natural place in the cosmos. We would hear them telling us from their own personal experiences that a greater perspective is possible. Evidence of higher consciousness exists from all ages in all civilizations, past and present, on this planet. The emphasis so far for humanity has tended toward a preoccupation with separatism, egotism, and, as we approach modern times, increased materialism in the West and now in the East.

In all of my academic studies, I discovered that there indeed existed this "other body of knowledge," and it appears that man has known of it for thousands of centuries. It seems that the keys to this "higher knowledge" and accurate information concerning the nature of energy and the life force have been available for many eons.

How and when did it all start? Where did this knowledge come from? Even modern man in all his apparent sophistication has not unraveled the mysteries of his origin, his world, and his universe. More and more evidence is being discovered indicating that some ancient peoples had a great deal of scientific knowledge which is accurate according to observations of twentieth-century new physics. In *Mysticism and the New Physics,* Michael Talbot states, "There are many parallel concepts between the ancient philosophies of the East and the emerging philosophies of the West. Certain concepts are so similar that it becomes impossible to discern whether some statements were made by the mystic or the physicist."

Mankind has always had a body of knowledge, often called ageless wisdom, which was passed on by word of mouth by teachers, priests, heroes, and other individuals. In man's later development, these inner knowledges explaining the mysteries of life and revealing the so-called "secrets" of universal laws were written and stored in many forms. A complex system of symbols, colors, and sounds developed. As the centuries passed, man focused increased attention on the gains of his ego and of the material world. To prevent misuse of power, the wisdom teachings were carefully hidden in veiled and abstruse language.

Throughout its long history, the knowledge of what is called in modern times "Reiki" has been passed from teacher to student by word of mouth. The origins of Reiki can be found in ancient Tibet many, many thousands of years ago. The ancient Tibetans had a knowledge and understanding of the essence of matter and energy which is only now being reflected in the discoveries of new physics. When Einstein, himself, in the formula $E = MC^2$ proclaimed that light and matter are interchangeable, he rediscovered what mystics seem to have known for centuries. Now the scientist becomes the mystic. Einstein reveals to the listening ear his inner process with his words, "I did not arrive at my understanding of the fundamental laws of the universe through my rational mind."

It appears that this knowledge of how to tap universal life-force energy eventually traveled from Tibet into India. From India, it was dispersed in many outer forms into the West through Egypt, Greece, and Rome. The ancient mystery schools guarded and protected this inner knowledge. Access to this knowledge was limited to the specially selected, to the elite, and to the privileged classes. Modern scholars often come upon this inner knowledge but misinterpret it because it was veiled in cryptic languages and symbols designed to give double meanings.

In the East, this knowledge was taken into China and Japan and also put into many other forms, hidden in symbols and buried in ancient, obscure languages.

Where mankind got this information originally still remains a mystery. In *The Sirius Mystery,* astronomer Robert Temple gives a scholarly, honest, yet cautious account of an anthropological study of the Dogon tribe in Africa, who have an incredible knowledge of Sirius, known as the Dog Star. In our remote past, has there been some contact with beings of a higher intelligence and consciousness who transmitted this knowledge of activating higher circuits in humans? Indeed, there is certainly strong evidence on this planet that some type of contact has been made.

Everyone has the ability to tap universal energy to some degree. It is obvious to everyone alive on this plane that all of us are in touch with life-force energy through our breath. In addition, we are also able to transmit to each other life energy in the power of our touch. Some people are able to send energy to others in thought forms. In ancient times, there were known keys to activate and to attune this natural energy within us and to lift our consciousness to a higher circuit.

In approximately the mid-nineteenth century, Dr. Mikao Usui rediscovered in some ancient texts the keys that act as a catalyst for releasing this natural energy. Later in his life, he called this precise technique for activating and tapping natural energy and the scientific method of applying or directing this energy "Reiki."

The story of Dr. Usui's search for this knowledge would best be described as a legend. As is often true of our unfolding life process and events in the past, detailed records were not kept. The essence of Dr. Usui's story, however, is that of a person searching, as so many are today, for contact with inner truth and enlightenment.

According to the legend, Dr. Usui was a scholar who had become a Christian minister and was teaching in a seminary in Kyoto, Japan. Both he and his students had been taught that in the past healing could be done by use of the power in one's hands. But Dr. Usui did not know how to teach this technique. After deep inner searching, he resigned from the school and came to America, hoping to find the knowledge he was lacking. He was not successful.

He returned to Japan and later traveled to India. Dr. Usui was able to read Sanscrit, an ancient language of India known by relatively few people today. In his searching and in his personal dedication to this mission, he eventually found the keys to this special knowledge preserved in Sanscrit as a formula. This formula is based on a series of symbols, which, when set into motion, activate and tap universal energy. It should certainly be no surprise to any of us that this knowledge could be regained since it had been known for thousands of years in various forms. It has been modern man's great loss to have lost contact with this knowledge and with this connection.

An analogy can be drawn with Einstein's modern formula revealing the profound scientific discovery that matter and energy are interchangeable. He wrote this formula in symbolic language—$E = MC^2$—and left instructions on how to use this knowledge and how to expand on it.

Consider for a moment that during the course of the next ten thousand years many civilizations will have risen and fallen. Knowledge that is available at this time will have been lost, destroyed, and buried. It is important to remember that the working knowledge $E = MC^2$ today is known by only a few people and truly understood by even fewer. Today a few people even know how to activate $E = MC^2$ into forms of energy called atomic bombs and a variety of other such devices.

To continue with our analogy, let us consider that a number of people had heard of this knowledge but only a few used it, learned from it, and preserved it. In the course of passing centuries, the formula $E = MC^2$ somehow has gotten lost. Then, one day in the year 11,981, someone rediscovers the formula $E = MC^2$ and the instructions on how to use it.

It happens that $E = MC^2$ is also a formula for tapping universal energy just as is the one rediscovered by Dr. Usui. The instructions he also discovered included directions on how to apply this life-force energy to all parts of your living being. In fact, these instructions give a precise, scientific method that can be used for healing or wholing oneself using natural energy and/or for activating higher circuits of consciousness.

Dr. Usui called this technique and process "Reiki," a Japanese word meaning universal life energy. To activate a higher level of natural energy according to the Reiki formula, one needs only a living transmitter and a living receiver. That is, the transmission or attunement is done by one person to another person. The person doing the transmission has mastered the knowledge preserved in the formulas discovered by Dr. Usui.

In the last years of his life, Dr. Usui taught this knowledge to several persons in Japan, who were then known as Reiki Masters. The method of teaching and preserving this knowledge was passed from teacher to student by word of mouth. A true Reiki Master has received a series of transmissions of energy and is able to activate energy in others. Certified Reiki Masters can also instruct others in how to apply this scientific method once the energy has been activated.

In the mid-1930s, an American-born woman of Japanese descent, who had been born in 1900 in the Hawaiian Islands, traveled to Japan. Her name was Hawayo Takata. She was a widow with two small daughters. Her health had deteriorated to a severely debilitating state. She returned to her parents' home in Japan to prepare for death and to leave her daughters in the care of her family.

During the weeks and months she was in Japan, she was told of a Reiki natural healing clinic in Tokyo. She found this clinic and immediately began a series of Reiki treatments that lasted for seven or eight months. She went to the Reiki clinic daily and received the precise Reiki treatment administered by two Reiki practitioners. After about eight months, Mrs. Takata's health was restored and her life energy renewed.

This experience was the turning point in her life. Not only had she been healed, but she had come in contact with a profound and real natural energy source that had transformed her physically, emotionally, mentally, and spiritually. With Reiki, her life had been saved and without surgery. Her wish now was to learn the Reiki method herself so that she could assist others in relieving suffering and give them the opportunity to obtain the wisdom one gains in using this profound technique.

In her remaining years in Japan, Takata was taught Reiki. She gained experience in using Reiki by working with people at the clinic. In the late 1930s, she returned to her home in Hawaii and began on a new course of her life.

Hers is a simple yet dramatic story of one woman's determination to help in the process of healing others. Some months later, she became a Reiki Master able to teach this wonderful technique to others and to fulfill her dream.

Over the next years, Takata taught Reiki, mainly in the remote interior of the Hawaiian Islands. Having had no formal education beyond the second or third grade, she relied upon a natural intelligence to spread her knowledge. Intuitively, she knew the profound depths of Reiki even though she lacked scientific and academic knowledge. Not until approximately 1975, when she was seventy-five, did she instruct others in the knowledge of how to activate this energy of a higher order. In 1980, Hawayo Takata died.

Takata told me the details of Dr. Usui's legend. Takata, however, never met Dr. Usui because he died many years before she went to Japan and was introduced to Reiki. Her retelling of his story was a long, involved, dramatically highlighted, and somewhat speculative third- or fourth hand account. In keeping with the purposes of this book, I have given an outline of what seem to be some of the events in the rediscovery of this profound ancient technique. The most important event is that this unique method was refound and called "Reiki" by Dr. Usui.

Takata acted as a bridge making available in the West a lost knowledge and healing art and science in the form of Reiki. Reiki has now reemerged as a new tool. Dr. Usui was the catalyst without whom the rediscovery of this knowledge would not have happened where it did.

My own academic background, specializing in classical civilizations and languages and including studies of ancient Egypt and Near Eastern civilizations, enabled me to recognize what, in its essence, Reiki really is. This knowledge enabled me to identify Reiki, to share this information with others who might not have studied mankind's past in such detail, and to put this information into a contemporary perspective free of outer trappings of limiting dogma. As I have mentioned earlier, this knowledge can be traced back thousands of years to Tibet. It has now resurfaced in the form of "Reiki" to be claimed by all of us as we progress into mankind's New Age, as we restore our power, and as we learn to heal and whole ourselves.

In the opening chapters of this book, I referred to the New Age of humanity that is in the process of birthing. One of the hallmarks of this New Age is that knowledge of how to reach health, wholeness, and enlightenment is available to anyone interested in gaining it and is not limited to an elite, select few. Humanity as a whole is in a profound process of making a transition from one stage of development to another—from one level of consciousness to another.

Reiki is an ancient knowledge brought forth for the New Age by Dr. Usui. It is both a profound tool for growth and transformation and a gentle, subtle, yet powerful healing and wholing art and science. Reiki gives you a direct way of contacting and applying natural energy. No words are adequate to describe fully the wisdom you will gain from the use of Reiki in your daily life.

PART II

Health is a precious thing . . . the only thing indeed that deserves to be pursued at the expense not only of time, sweat, labor, worldly goods but of life itself; since without health life becomes a burden and an affliction.

Montaigne

9

Reiki in Your Daily Life

*Any imbalance is experienced as a need
to correct this imbalance.*
Frederick S. Perls

Reiki is a technique for activating universal life energy of a higher order within you, and it is a specific method for applying this energy and balancing yourself and healing yourself. One of the basic tenets of wholistic health and living is accepting responsibility for your own health, sense of well-being, and evolving consciousness. Reiki is a unique method for unlocking the powers that can be found within all of us, and Reiki can be easily used in your daily life in numerous ways. The Reiki method gives you a direct means of restoring vital energy as you deplete energy during your daily activities, whatever they may be. Depleting or exhausting your vital energy throughout the day *without* adequately and fully replenishing it results in imbalances that affect your physical, emotional, mental, spiritual dynamic.

Reiki is *not* a substitute for your need to restore energy with natural foods, nor is it a substitute for exercise appropriate to your particular lifestyle. Reiki is, however, an essential source of natural energy that enhances all of your activities. For example, many runners and other athletes have taken the Reiki

Seminar to restore energy burned up in sports and other exercise activities.

Reiki can be used on the spot to energize yourself no matter where you are or what you are doing. Reiki can be used effectively in balancing your energy physically, emotionally, and mentally as you progress through daily situations and inter- actions. Reiki is also effective in eliminating or controlling the effects of bruises, bumps, burns, and bleeding from cuts or other accidents that might happen to you in the course of daily activities.

Headaches are one of the most common complaints in our contemporary society. Studies show that Americans consume millions of aspirins and other pain-relief pills each day. The feedback I get most frequently about Reiki is its effectiveness in releasing headaches and other pain. Migraines respond pos- itively when Reiki is used consistently over a period of several weeks or months, and the migraine pattern can usually be elim- inated completely with Reiki, when used as instructed. Head- aches are important signals of accumulated negative stress or imbalanced energy. Reiki promotes negative stress release and energy balancing as well as positive stress responses so that you are healing the cause and eliminating the effect.

Once you have learned the Reiki technique, you will be able to apply its basic principles to any disease or energy imbalance you are experiencing in the daily course of your life. With Reiki, it is possible to obtain relief from allergies, arthritis, and other chronic imbalances. By using Reiki *as instructed,* it is possible to build a high level of reserve energy so that during more distressful times in your life you will have something to "fall back on" without completely draining yourself. With Reiki, your natural resiliency is enhanced. Continual depletion of vital energy without replenishing it adequately tends to run down your immune system. The immune system is the body's natural defense against disease. Reiki gives you a technique effective in balancing and enhancing the immune system.

Part II of this book gives some specific uses of Reiki in

promoting energy balancing, healing, wholing, and positive well-ness. Since researchers now are able to relate high levels of negative stress to deficient immune systems tending to result in disease and imbalances, special attention is given to stress, relaxation, and Reiki. Releasing and reducing negative stress while promoting positive stress responses appears to be an essential *key* to balanced energy, positive wellness, wholeness, and even enlightenment. Keep in mind as you are reading that *all of the principles* of using Reiki *apply* to *all* diseases and imbalances *whether or not* I make a specific reference to one that is of special interest to you. Reiki is a universal life energy, and the technique can be applied safely to any living organism. These chapters also provide other examples of benefits received by individuals with Reiki, whether it was used alone or in combination with medical treatments and/or other therapies.

The chapter on death, dying and Reiki is intended to help you understand the dying and death process as a natural and highly significant part of each of our lives. One of the first and perhaps the most difficult lessons in healing and wholing is that of letting go of rigid attachments to expectations and end results. Life is a *process, not a result.* Healing, wholing, and balancing energy is a process, and dying is a natural part of the life experience. Dying and renewing or rebirthing into other states of being are natural cycles within which our whole life experience exists. Reiki is an ancient wisdom that can be used now to support and to help guide ourselves and others through the dying process.

Reiki goes along *naturally* with whatever your own individual process is in the "here-now." The key to immortality is in awakening consciousness, not in holding onto outer forms, limited patterns, or closed systems, whether they be physical, emotional, or mental. A step in awakening your consciousness is *trusting* in your life's unfolding process, expressed in con-temporary jargon, "going with the flow." Reiki is a special technique that helps you *where you are* and gently beckons you to opening each day of your life.

Here is a wonderful Sufi tale for reflection:

*The great Sufi sage, Mullah Nasrudin, once entered a shop
and demanded of the keeper, "Have you ever seen me before?" "No!" responded the shopkeeper promptly. "Then,"
cried Nasrudin, "how do you know it is me?"*

10

Stress, Relaxation, and Reiki

*There are two roads to survival: fight
and adaptation. And most often adaptation is the more successful.*
Hans Selye

Stress as defined by medical researchers describes the daily
wear and tear on our bodies, emotions, minds, and spirits. Dr.
Hans Selye, director of the Institute on Experimental Medicine
and Surgery at the University of Montreal and the leading
authority on stress, defines stress "as the body's nonspecific
response to any demand made upon it."[1] In and of itself, the
stress response is neither good nor bad, and Dr. Selye's definition
clearly shows that the stress response cannot be eliminated.
Stress, however, can be divided into two basic categories:
positive stress responses, which bring us joy, balance, wellness,
and wholeness, and negative stress responses, which Dr. Selye
calls *distress,* which drain your energy, sap your vitality, lower
your resistance, and make you vulnerable to disease on all levels
of your being. Current research indicates that when distress is
prolonged or excessive in your life, you begin suffering from
physical, emotional, and mental disharmonies. You age pre-
maturely, and you could experience chronic, dehabilitating,
physical conditions. Emotionally, you lose your ability to cope.

59

You suffer anxiety, depression, fatigue, and irritability. Mentally, you become confused and unable to think clearly and to make choices and decisions rationally. Spiritually, you feel empty inside, bored, cynical, and, essentially, unfulfilled. Stress can accumulate to such an extent that a person can no longer cope and illnesses develop. Research on the relationship between stress and disease over many years has shown that a connection does exist.

Dr. Herbert Benson, in his book *The Relaxation Response,* points out that the human nervous system is designed to handle certain amounts of stress. The nervous system is set to react to external threats in what has been termed the "fight or flight" response. Modern man, however, often finds himself in many situations in which he inhibits his natural fight or flight response. When your boss ridicules your work, or a spouse or parent constantly attacks you verbally, or any other number of external demands are put on you daily, your body has a distress response. Unfortunately, in many of these situations, fight or flight is not appropriate. Consequently, you constantly suppress your responses to stress. What results is chronic distress, stress that is held in and not released. As Dr. Carl Simonton, leading authority in cancer research, puts it, "And chronic stress, it is increasingly recognized, plays a significant role in many illnesses."[2]

Dr. Harold Bloomfield, a leading exponent of the wholistic approach, lists the major symptoms of excessive stress as including difficulty falling asleep or sleeping through the night, tension headaches, free-floating anxiety, feeling all wound up, feeling down in the dumps, chronic fatigue, pouches or dark circles under eyes, worry, inability to concentrate, irritability, frequent indigestion, frequent constipation, frequent colds, frequent angry outbursts, and excessive drinking, smoking and eating. Certain bodily changes accompany unreleased distress and have a detrimental, sometimes devastating, effect on our health and sense of well-being. These changes include internal chemical reactions, hormonal changes, muscular tensions, increased heart rate, accelerated breathing, circulation difficulties, tension to our internal glands and organs, anxiety, and depression. There is much evidence to demonstrate the physical effects of stress. And, in addition, Dr. Selye's research has shown a definite connection between emotional and mental chronic stress and suppression or deterioration of the immune system. Without doubt, there is a significant link between our physical, emotional, mental, and spiritual bodies. Physical distress tends to trigger emotional and mental distress and vice versa.

In our modern societies, we have to learn how to deal with distress-causing elements in our daily lives. First, we need to learn how to identify *what is causing* our negative stress accumulation. Our physical environment itself can be a high-level source of negative stress. External factors such as polluted air, food, and water, overcrowded conditions, and high noise levels increase our distress. Take, for example, the issue of noise and stress. Most of us experience the constant noise from motorized vehicles and machines. There are the sounds of people everywhere, of doors slamming, cars screeching, and planes flying overhead. In our homes and those of our neighbors, there are fairly constant noises from televisions, stereos, radios, and an unbelievable assortment of rumbling appliances, some of which never turn off, as well as the persistent ringing of telephones. Likewise, we must take into consideration that our emotional responses to high-level, constant noise can also be distressful. Typical responses are anger, irritation, aggressiveness, frustration, and anxiety.

Studies have shown that high-density and/or prolonged noises can be devastating to our wholeness. Dr. Dale Hattis of Massachusetts Institute of Technology concluded that "loud noises may increase the adhesiveness of platelets in the blood to each other and that may contribute to long-term chronic arteriosclerosis—hardening of the arteries."[3]

Noise level and constancy as a source of distress in our daily lives is obviously just one area of our environment we would need to consider in assessing stress factors affecting each one of us.

In following a wholistic approach to health and living, you

would examine all possible distress factors in your life. You should include not only your physical environment but also your personal relationships, your basic attitudes about life and your fellowman, your job or career activities, and your personal interests. I recommend that you begin now. Make a list of the negative stress-related symptoms you tend to exhibit most frequently. Then, begin a list of possible *causes* for these symptoms. Include physical as well as emotional, mental, and spiritual causes. In this process, you are beginning your personal journey in searching for Self. Working with finding the causes of blocks or distress that could be keeping you from your own, unique, self-actualizing process begins another level of personal growth and expression for you. Discovering who you really are, getting in touch with your true self, expanding your sphere of consciousness, and *consciously* becoming one with your source is an incredibly sacred, beautiful journey toward wholeness.

In this process, you will need appropriate techniques designed inherently to promote positive stress responses and to help you release the effects of accumulated negative stress when the basic fight or flight response is not socially acceptable. In reference to dealing with stress, Dr. Simonton stated, "The key is the need to adapt to *change,* whether or not that change is in a positive or negative direction."⁴ Physically, you will be moving toward a level of fitness suitable to your needs. You will be learning to renew and sustain a balance of natural energy. Emotionally, you will be moving toward a sense of well-being, an intrinsic happiness, and experiences of confidence, spontaneity, and optimism. You will be moving away from constant depression, anger, worry, and anxiety. Mentally, you will be expanding to clarity in thinking, and you will be healing old fears, inhibitions, and hang-ups, and you will be learning to deal with stress in new ways. Spiritually, you will be opening the doors to a wider sphere of consciousness. You will be expanding to touching directly into your source of unconditional love, of unlimited strength, and of compassion. You will be becoming the authentic, genuine, real you!

The technique of Reiki is, in and of itself, complete and

one that promotes distress releasing and full relaxation, both externally and internally. In the process of using Reiki, you are *naturally,* without force or without any artificial means, promoting positive stress responses throughout your entire being. Simultaneously, by doing the Reiki treatment each day, you are releasing accumulated negative stress.

One woman, Dorothy,* had been undergoing dramatic changes in her life. Within seven months, she had lost her husband in a job-related accident and her youngest son to leukemia. When she came to the Reiki Seminar, she was visibly exhausted and had dark circles and big bags under her eyes. Her vitality level was extremely low, and her health had been deteriorating at a rapid rate. She began using Reiki as instructed on a daily basis. She had been to several doctors and one chiropractor and had tried psychotherapy for several months. Nothing seemed to help. At this point, her enthusiasm for Reiki left much to be desired, but a friend had suggested the technique to her. She was so low that she had nothing to lose. As instructed, she began using Reiki on a daily basis—sometimes several times a day. Within two weeks, the change in her appearance and attitude was so profound that even her friends had difficulty recognizing her. She has been using Reiki for nearly two years now. She says that with Reiki she was able to change her response, gradually to release distress accumulated throughout her life, to benefit more from her psychotherapy, and to create a new, stimulating, and fulfilling cycle in her life.

Reiki is vital, life, light-energy, and in the series of transmissions given in the Reiki Seminar your ability to tap this source energy is natural, direct, and amplified. The *connection* is made every single time as long as you are touching into something that is *alive*—be it yourself, a loved one, a pet, or plants. Once you have received the authentic Reiki transmissions, absolutely *nothing* can interfere with your new ability to tap life, light-energy as long as the receiver is alive and as long as you

*In most cases, pseudonyms (fictitious names) have been used to protect individual privacy. In every other aspect, the facts of the cases are unchanged.

64 THE REIKI FACTOR

actually use the technique. With Reiki, you will be carrying with you *at all times* and in every situation and location a technique that can be used on the spot for stress releasing. In addition, Reiki promotes energy-balancing, energy-renewing, positive stress responses and gives *the key* to adapting to change in your life, whether that change is negative or positive.

When distress is accumulated in your system as a result of the rigors of modern life, personal relationships, and life's process itself, you can use your Reiki for a few minutes in your office, in your car, riding on a bus, in a grocery store, while standing in lines, or virtually anywhere. Reiki requires no special equipment, no altered states of consciousness, no special preparations or clothes, and no special moods or locations. Reiki is not a dogma, not a religion, and not dependent on whether or not you believe in it. When this energy connection is put into motion, it works automatically just as your breath works without your thoughts or belief. At your birth, you were moved from one environment to another, and a connection was made with life on this plane. In a similar way, Reiki amplifies the connection with universal energy, focuses the energy flow through your hands (although other focus points have been used, such as feet), and provides a specific technique that promotes positive stress responses and consciousness expansion and supports your process toward wholeness. Reiki is energy, and energy, ultimately, is light. Reiki literally puts you in direct contact with the Light and lets you apply this light-energy from the outside, physically, to the inside.

A legal secretary began using Reiki to help some of the attorneys in her office with muscular tensions, headaches, and other distress symptoms such as frustration, fatigue, and irritability. After a couple of weeks, everyone in this office of four top Atlanta attorneys, three legal secretaries, and one receptionist noticed a profound difference in attitude; all had increased energy levels and increased ability to cope with daily stress factors. She reported that the atmosphere in the entire office changed. It was not as "heavy" as it had been and seemed "light." With Reiki so much in demand, she began losing

her coffee break time and lunch hour. One of the attorneys nick-
named it "Ramaki." Finally, she suggested that each of them
take the Reiki Seminar, so that each could use the technique
directly without relying on her.

One young man, who commutes to work in New York by
subway each day, wrote to thank me for the Reiki Seminar.
He reported that he began using Reiki during his thirty-minute
subway ride going to and from work. He stated further, "I
was amazed at the relief I got from anxiety about my job,
about going to that office and dealing with my co-workers.
My general energy level increased. Each evening while riding
home and doing Reiki, I seemed to regenerate myself and I
would arrive home feeling relaxed. It definitely had a positive
effect on my family life."

Consider the following letter, reprinted in full, written by a
successful businesswoman in Atlanta:

*I want to thank you again for the two Reiki treatments I
have had to date. I honestly did not believe the process
would work; my first reaction was that Reiki was only a sort
of metaphysical placebo and therefore couldn't possibly be
effective on me as I tend to be much more pragmatic. As
you recall, when I came to you for my first treatment, I was
suffering the conglomerate of ill symptoms that has been
best termed "executive stress"—I was exhausted, my entire
body ached, my mind was disorganized, I was emotionally
drained, and I felt a little nauseous. I was too tired to sleep.
I was having difficulty handling my business operations
efficiently. After an hour of treatment, the nausea was
gone, my mental clarity had returned, and I felt energetic,
objective, relaxed, and filled with a new sense of purpose. I
went home and was able to plan a new administrative
strategy which has greatly enhanced my business operations.
It was as though you had put me in touch with the best of
myself. Thank you again for the treatments. Reiki should
be available through every medical, chiropractic and mental
health facility in this country. Your fees are a small price to
pay for such impressive results. I don't know how Reiki
works, but it works; that's all that counts in my book.*

One evening I stopped by a hospital to give one of my

clients a Reiki treatment before her surgery the next morning. A tumor had been discovered in her uterus, cancer was suspected, and she would be undergoing a complete hysterectomy. When I entered her room, I noticed immediately her radiance and calmness. She told me she had been doing Reiki on herself all afternoon amid the blood tests and physical preparations. From inside, fear, anxiety, depression, and terror had begun to get a hold on her. Then she remembered what I had instructed in the Reiki Seminar—always use your Reiki in highly distressful situations, *no matter where you are.* With Reiki, she could feel herself stabilizing emotionally and mentally almost immediately. She became interested in the preparatory activities, she relaxed, she was participating, she was even able to laugh more objectively at some of the routine procedures, and she talked with one of the attending nurses about Reiki.

After the surgery, the woman kept on doing Reiki. I visited her two more times, and she was thrilled with her positive recovery process with Reiki. She was aware of the renewed, vital energy being restored in her system. She knew she was healing and wholing on all levels of her being. She commented that she had never been so relaxed in her life, and yet she was in a hospital undergoing major surgery. It was a *real* growth process for her!

One woman from Smyrna, Georgia, whose entire family, including her husband, a ten-year-old, and an eight-year-old son, took the Reiki Seminar, wrote:

> *When I use the Reiki, I get very sleepy and relaxed. Sometimes I will go to sleep in the middle of the Reiki treatment. I am not one to see things or to hear things that are not there but, during some of the Reiki treatments I see WHITE light in various forms. . . . [my husband] gets immediate relief for his headaches with the Reiki*

Another woman wrote the following letter:

> *It seems that there was hardly a day I can remember that I wasn't stressed and anxious. I had a chronic bladder infection and off and on suffered from severe migraine head-*

*aches. I knew those conditions were not normal but even
modern medicine and psychiatry didn't seem to help.*

*I felt helpless and often hopeless. The quality of my
life and vitality was at a minimum and my life had but
little meaning. I heard about Reiki and hoped it would
help my bladder. Well, it did more than that. I was a
changed person. My anxiety level went down, my migraines
decreased and my appreciation for life increased a hundred-
fold. I laughed more, was less tense and was much more
patient with myself and others. I love the Reiki treatments
I give myself . . . it is the highlight of my day.*

One man in his mid-thirties who took Reiki told the class that
he worked a day job as well as an evening job in order to
support his family and cope with inflation. He was, however,
exhausted. A friend who had received enormous benefits from
the Reiki technique had recommended the seminar to him. He
was totally skeptical about it, but he was *sure* that he was
tired of being tired. After the first Reiki transmission and
instructions, he left for his all-night job. The next afternoon,
he came to the class very excited. He said that he had nearly
fallen asleep on the job, but, as soon as he did some Reiki,
he could feel his energy being restored. In thirty hours, he had
managed to get only four hours sleep but found he could again
stabilize and reenergize himself in twenty minutes with Reiki.
He told us that Reiki reminded him of the statement in a TV
commercial for batteries, which ended with "energize me."

A student in his mid-thirties at a local university reported
that with Reiki he could concentrate more completely on his
assignments and was doing much better in test situations, which
usually triggered in him anxiety, tenseness, and mental blocking.
By doing fifteen minutes of Reiki before tests, he found his
anxiety diminished, his mind cleared, and his confidence enhanced. He is also involved in sports and found Reiki helpful
on the spot for strains, bruises, tensions, and centering himself.

A young woman had a nervous disposition, involving tension
and anxiety, and developing nearly daily severe headaches. Her
father-in-law had benefited enormously from Reiki and recommended she take the seminar. Within only two weeks after she

completed the course, everyone she knew was amazed at the positive transformation in her personality. She was relaxed, was coping entirely differently with her family and friends, and was free from the tension and pain caused by the formerly severe headaches. She said that Reiki was practical, effective, simple to use, did not require extra money for additional accessories, and did not cause conflicts with her husband. She was sure that Reiki had resulted in her personal transformation because nothing else new had been introduced into her life. She said Reiki had given her "peace inside."

One of the additional positive benefits of Reiki is that it can be used *along with* medical therapies and other techniques for healing and wholing. I have taught Reiki to many medical doctors, to osteopaths, to chiropractors, to massage experts, to dentists, to nurses, and to many others involved in various aspects of health care. One man, who had been a transcendental meditator, found Reiki "most enlightening" when used with his mantra. An expert yoga instructor verified that she combined Reiki with some of the yoga positions and found her experiences more vivid, even more profound—"truly spiritual and enlightening."

A Rolfer found that Reiki added a "special powerful but gentle" touch to his rolfing technique. A medical doctor said that with Reiki he is able to transmit healing energy directly to his patients now even while talking with them. Another medical doctor reported that, in just a few minutes with Reiki, he could reduce a patient's stress responses of tension, anxiety, and pain. Many psychologists have found Reiki to be indispensable in helping to calm a patient in any anxiety attack and in promoting trust in the special relationship between client and therapist. Many cancer patients have found Reiki to be extremely effective in diminishing and, in some cases, in eliminating the often devastating side effects of radiation, chemotherapy, and other drugs. Many have used Reiki to restore natural energy depleted by drugs, surgery, and long or chronic illnesses. Reiki in *no way* conflicts with medical procedures but rather offers an often badly needed source of vital energy to help promote the healing process.

Not only is Reiki a beneficial technique that can be used in combination with other methods, but it also can be applied while you are watching television, talking on the phone, meeting with others, and even resting. I have gotten into the habit of doing Reiki now when I am watching the evening news programs, which often are filled with distressful commentaries on our modern society! One woman expressed it this way, "No matter where I am or what I am doing, I work in a little Reiki on myself. At my company's weekly business meeting, which is always highly pressured, highly tense, and highly charged, I stay relaxed, stress-free, and clear-headed while everyone else gets angry, anxious, and tense. I used to leave those meetings with severe headaches but now I do Reiki, respond and interact calmly, and leave the meeting feeling good!"

One of the most relaxing and negative-stress-releasing combinations I have found and strongly recommend for promoting stress responses, healing, and wholeness is that of doing Reiki while listening to certain music. For example, Steven Halpern, a nationally known composer, creates what he has termed "anti-frantic" music. His scientific approach to music results in the creation of sounds that are designed to resonate to the natural harmony and life force within our cells. He states, "Because all activity involves stress . . . the body will need to readjust back to a sense of normalcy, or homeostasis, of balance. In other words, *the body seeks to get in 'harmony with itself.'* "[5] With his kind of music or with chants and meditation tones and with Reiki, you will be giving yourself a bath of light and vibrational energy that promotes healing and wholeness. It is, indeed, an incredible experience as well as being a highly efficient, relatively low-cost, and extremely practical method of releasing negativity from your entire being rather than storing it in your system for weeks, even years, resulting in premature degeneration, aging, chronic and terminal illness, and constant fatigue. A vacation once a year for relaxing and resting is not sufficient for adequate releasing of distress caused by the extra-ordinary pace of our daily lives, by old emotional patterns stored deep within, perhaps from childhood, by rigid, narrow thinking, and by spiritual feelings of inner emptiness and futility.

One of the hallmarks of wholistic health and living is the tenet that *you* assume responsibility for your wellness and wholeness. The truth is that it is not up to someone else to keep you well, nor is personal lack of wellness and wholeness always someone else's fault. Reiki gives you an opportunity to assume this responsibility, privately, in your way, according to your own needs, as well as in conjunction with family and friends.

Health, wellness, and wholeness require the integrating of body, emotions, mind, and spirit. Dr. Harold Bloomfield reminds us that "positive wellness rather than the mere absence of symptoms must be the goal of health care."[6] In the Reiki Seminars, I express it this way: "Remember always that health and wholeness are your divine birthright, which you have the *right* to claim now." Reiki is a direct, natural source of the light-energy of life for restoring, renewing, transforming, and transmuting energy in your personal, unfolding process of life. Reiki is a technique that can be used by individuals of all ages to deal with distress and to promote positive stress responses. By using Reiki, you are acknowledging your own involvement and direct participation in your healing or wholing process. With Reiki, you are activating in a new, efficient way your power within for releasing negative stress accumulations, for balancing and renewing your energy and vitality, and for maintaining your health and wholeness.

11

Cancer and Reiki

It is a particularly sad course of events, that many times those people who most steadfastly and responsibly attempt to live up to cultural rules develop the most serious illnesses. The literature is replete with examples characterizing cancer patients in general as "too good to be true" —people who are kind, considerate, unselfish and pleasant in the face of all adversity. . . . Individuals who begin to accept responsibility for influencing the state of their health deserve the greatest of congratulations.

**Carl and Stephanie Simonton
and James Creighton**

In the Reiki Seminars which I teach, one of the most frequently asked questions is, "How can Reiki help with cancer?" Many of those who take the Reiki Seminar do so because either they or someone close to them is dealing with some form of cancer.

The Reiki technique can be helpful in significant ways in the healing or wholing process of cancer patients. One of the most common problems with cancer and with techniques such as

71

chemotherapy, radiation, and surgery is the energy-draining, loss-of-vitality effect on cancer patients. In many cases, the person must select one or more of these current cancer-treating techniques even though the side effects can be devastating and healing results are not certain. Reiki can be used effectively with whatever therapies the person is undergoing. Reiki gives an immediate, direct, amplified contact with natural, vital light-energy. Reiki can in no way interfere with the traditional medical approaches, but it can give the patient an often badly needed source of natural energy for restoring energy loss and for promoting the healing process.

Reiki is also highly effective in dealing with the extreme physical pain often associated with cancer. In addition, Reiki helps the cancer patient to deal with emotional responses such as fear, depression, and anger. Many cancer patients who have taken Reiki have found this source of light-energy to be spiritually uplifting and to be an essential tool in helping to prepare for the dying process in so-called "terminal" situations.

One of the most profound and enlightening experiences I have had with Reiki and with a cancer patient began several years ago in a northern city. After hearing the introductory lecture on Reiki, a woman who appeared to be in her early fifties approached the speaker's podium. She explained that several years earlier she had battled with cancer, had won a reprieve, but now was suffering from a recurrence of the disease. Medical examinations revealed that the cancer had spread throughout her entire lympathic system, had invaded her brain, and had spread into her bone marrow. She had been diagnosed as being terminal and had been given only a few months to live. She explained further that she had tried a large number of healing techniques in addition to the chemotherapy and radiation. As she put it, "I have gone from A to Z to try to discover why I am dying of cancer and to find techniques appropriate in my healing process. I have even tried past-life regression to find the causes, but I still do not understand 'why.'" Then she looked at me with intense, piercing eyes and in a challenging tone asked me what

Reiki could do for her. I held her gaze momentarily, looking deep within her, and responded, "Reiki will help you with your pain." She admitted that she had been disillusioned with many techniques. She left the lecture without committing herself to take the class. The next morning she came with a friend to the Reiki Seminar. During the break, Janet shared with me that her physical pain was so intense that she was taking eight to ten prescription pain pills a day. She was angry, she said, because she was even missing her own dying process because the pain pills blurred and dulled her mind.

After the first Reiki activating energy transmission, Janet's face took on a new radiance. Her eyes began to sparkle and her facial skin, which had been dull and gray, was restored to color and brightness. In the seminar, we discussed the dying process and the importance of being in tune with this experience. She began to see a new dimension and to accept herself in a "new light." Later that week, she called the Reiki Center in Atlanta to tell me that, after only five days of Reiki, she was taking only two to four pain pills a day. She was amazed at how clear her mind was and how much vital energy was being restored to her extremely drained body with Reiki. She had been using the Reiki treatment on herself at least three times a day, and other friends who had taken the seminar were also giving her treatments.

As the weeks passed, Janet was able to reduce her need for pain pills to only one every several days. A few months later, I saw her again. She had changed dramatically. Her face was radiant, her energy level was high, she had gained some weight, her self-confidence was restored, and she had begun teaching her beloved yoga classes again. Janet was a giver and a healer, and with Reiki she was once again able to teach and give. She was also most impressed with how Reiki enhanced the mental imagery technique she had learned at Dr. Carl Simonton's clinic, which specializes in cancer research. In addition to the medical therapies, she considered Reiki and the Simonton mental imagery to be her most effective daily tools.

Janet attended my next lecture in her area and shared with

the audience how much the *quality* of her life had changed with Reiki, how effective Reiki was in pain relief but, most of all, how much spiritual inspiration and enlightenment she had gotten from her Reiki treatments.

For the next two years she kept in touch with me by telephone and by mail. Once she wrote that her doctor felt that something was being "reactivated," possibly in her brain. Since she had used Reiki, she had grown substantial amounts of her hair on her head. Her self-confidence in her appearance was restored, and her embarrassment at her baldness caused by the chemotherapy, radiation, and other drugs was diminished. She also said that she was glad to have taken the Reiki Second Degree because "it gives me much satisfaction to do distant healing . . . it is a good feeling to me to think that I have at least tried to be of help to others."

Early last fall, word came that Janet had died or, in New Age phraseology, had made her transition. Right to her last days on this plane, she had taught yoga and had lived a full and active life for nearly three years beyond what had been medically predicted. With Reiki, she had been able to dissipate her extreme depression. Most important, however, she had continued to learn, to grow, and to undergo profound physical, emotional, mental, and spiritual transformations. In the last months, she wrote to me, "I believe that I am doing as well as I am because of Reiki."

Janet had brought a wholistic approach into her consciousness and had reaped many benefits. She felt that the most important thing Reiki had given her was renewed vitality, a direct source for natural energy, and an inner strength and peace she had never before known. Indeed, her new light showed in her face, in her changed attitude, and in her determination to participate *actively and consciously* in this part of her own life process—wherever the journey was taking her. Her dying and death process was truly a beginning of a new cycle in her continuum of consciousness.

Janet's case has been discussed at length because it so clearly demonstrates the many levels of benefits possible from

Reiki for those persons dealing with cancer and with other extremely deenergizing diseases. In addition, her case raises the question, rhetorical though it may be, whether she could have healed the cancer if she had been able to use Reiki sooner. Too often, those who seek additional healing therapies do so in the terminal phase of the disease when even all the medical technologies have failed. When the alternative healing therapies also appear to fail, these techniques are then unfairly criticized, ridiculed, and dismissed as valueless. In this New Age of expanded awareness, however, each of us has the opportunity to perceive health matters from a larger perspective. This perspective, wholistic in nature, includes the outstanding advances of medical technology *as well as* other techniques that promote health, well-being, and wholeness on all levels of our being. With a wholistic perspective, you do not have to wait until you are "terminal" on this plane of existence to explore and use effectively wholeness-promoting techniques.

One of the most significant aspects of Janet's story is that with Reiki she became an *active* participant in her life process. She expressed to me that she no longer felt as helpless and personally devastated by the cancer. Inwardly, she grew, and the light-energy of Reiki opened the doors to deeper perceptions about her *process* and helped put her in contact with other dimensions of her being.

An eighty-three-year-old woman who had undergone surgery to remove a cancerous lump from her intestines was given the gift of Reiki by her concerned daughter. The daughter, who held a Ph.D. in psychology, and her husband, who was a practicing psychiatrist, had been benefiting from Reiki for nearly a year. Both were highly impressed with the results of Reiki on many levels. After surgery, her mother was getting chemotherapy weekly for approximately one year. At eighty-three, she had managed to keep a bright attitude about life and was open to learning something new. Accustomed to a high energy level all her life, she was aware of the enormous energy drain she experienced after each chemotherapy treatment. She also was apprehensive about the side effects often related to chemotherapy such as loss of hair, change in skin texture, and possible internal complications. After the Reiki class, she gave herself daily treatments as well as receiving Reiki from her daughter. She immediately noticed the positive change in her energy level with Reiki. Her face brightened, natural energy was restored where it had been depleted, and her fears were alleviated. She was able to release stress accumulated daily from taking care of herself and helping her ailing husband. After one year, she was taken off of chemotherapy, free of cancer. She still uses Reiki for restoring energy. In addition, she suffered no loss of hair and no other visible side effects from the chemotherapy.

At the Reiki Center in Atlanta and in my travels, I have worked with many women of all ages who are suffering from breast cancer. A woman in Detroit in her late twenties had undergone a radical mastectomy. Tests revealed that the cancer had spread to her lymphatic system, and the doctors were not optimistic in their assessment of the situation. She came to the Reiki class depressed, frightened, and extremely weak physically. She was on a regular program of radiation, and with two young children at home she was losing energy faster than it was being restored. With the first Reiki activating energy, her energy level increased dramatically. Others in the class could see the change in her energy right away. The heavy negativity surrounding her began to lighten. By the end of this first session, her cheeks were glowing and her eyes were shining.

During the next several days, we did Reiki on her during the classes. In a private session on the fourth day, she revealed how many transformations she had gone through just being in the class and then by doing three to five hours of Reiki on herself each day. The swelling and pain in her arm had been reduced greatly. She was beginning to think more clearly about ways to help herself and to promote healing. She said she was still terrified of death, but, when she was doing Reiki her fears diminished. She said she had seen "white light" being transmitted in each of the four Reiki activating energies I had done. She knew the road ahead would be difficult and many things were yet unresolved within her, but Reiki had restored her energy, released the pain, and restored her confidence. She felt she was on a new cycle.

Since that time, I have received letters from her telling about her continued use of Reiki, as instructed, and giving thanks for the opportunity to take the Reiki Seminar. She believes she *is healing* even though she has a long way to go, and Reiki was an essential ingredient in this healing process.

Another woman, in her sixties, rapidly developed a cancerous tumor in her left breast. She reported that her oncologist explained the critical nature of the situation. They agreed on surgery within a few days. She wrote to me, "My physician son soon contacted the Reiki Master in our city. She reacted instantly by sending Reiki absentee healing, which raised my energy, stabilized the emotions of my family and me, along with the added plus of peace of mind and heart during the various stages of preparation . . . my Reiki children-physician and wife together with a Reiki therapist (from the Reiki Center in Atlanta) gave me personal daily benefits."

At that time, my own schedule took me out of Atlanta. When I returned on Saturday, I went to Emory hospital to give her a Reiki treatment. The surgery had been done on the previous Tuesday. The entire breast had been removed as well as the node under her arm. To everyone's relief, the tests indicated no apparent spreading of the cancer. To everyone's surprise, the scar was healing *without* discoloration and without swelling. Her arm lacked even the usual puffiness associated with this surgery. She had received Reiki treatments both before and after surgery. With Reiki, her healing process had been accelerated. Her attending physician was very impressed with the results. She was released from the hospital after only five days instead of the usual ten. She returned to work within only one month. She said that her "energy buildup was unbelievable." A month later, both she and her husband took the Reiki class so that they could do Reiki for themselves and for each other. She wrote, "How blessed are those who have (1) received Reiki's benefits and (2) taken the next step—participation by preparation and practicing it in their lives daily."

Three years ago, a very frightened, desperate-sounding woman phoned me about the possibility of using Reiki to help with a severe cancerous disease that was recurring across her nose and cheeks. She had been advised by expert physicians at Emory University that the necessary surgery would be extremely painful and slow to heal. This extensive and complicated surgery was scheduled for three months from the time she called.

I immediately taught her Reiki as well as giving her regular treatments three times a week. She used Reiki on her face many hours each day—even at work she would sit with her hands cupping her face to get extra Reiki. She was truly surprised at the emotional and mental stability and peace of mind she was experiencing with Reiki. Two months later, she went to Emory for testing relating to the upcoming surgery. The doctors were amazed at the transformation in her condition. She was re-scheduled for less severe surgery from which she recovered more rapidly than had been expected. When I last heard from her, she said that she was using Reiki to transform some old, negative emotional patterns. She also said that without the Reiki light-energy her surgery would have been a much worse ordeal.

Recently, a twenty-six-year-old woman with advanced cancer of the stomach and lungs took the Reiki class. She came in physically weak and exhausted and emotionally depressed. She was having a great deal of difficulty dealing with her physical disease, with her energy depletion, with her three young children, with her marriage relationship, and with a full-time job. She told the class that she had been healthy and highly energetic all of her life, but the cancer had appeared suddenly and in an advanced stage.

She had almost completely given up any hope of living. She was deeply depressed and angered at her predicament. Since her usual energy level had been high, she could not believe how totally drained she felt after chemotherapy. With the first Reiki activating energy transmission, she could feel the natural energy flowing into her body. Her face brightened and her spirit elevated. During the last class, she told everyone that she managed to get in three to five hours of Reiki each day. As she put it, "I am a new person as far as my restored energy is concerned. I have a long way to go, but I feel so much less helpless with Reiki—I don't even resent the chemotherapy as much since I can do Reiki while receiving it."

The next account is of an incredible woman in her late forties who had worked both as a legal secretary and as a healer. She had studied and taught various forms of healing for nearly fifteen years. She began studying Reiki, taking both First and Second Degree, and offered her services to others as a Reiki therapist. Then, in the summer of 1980, she noticed a persistent sore throat and a small lump in the right side of her neck. Reiki took away the extreme soreness, but the lump had not subsided. She decided to use alternate methods for healing, but by mid-fall the lump had gotten larger and harder.

In October, I saw her and recommended that she go immediately to a medical doctor who was a close friend of mine and who combined medical techniques with other wholistic methods. He had also taken the Reiki Seminar and was familiar with the ways she could help with her own healing process. After a thorough examination, he sent her to a surgeon, and surgery was scheduled for December. During surgery, however, only the right tonsil could be removed. The lump was determined to be malignant. She was scheduled for eight weeks of radiation followed by surgery to remove the lump.

She had radiation treatments five days a week for eight weeks. In her words, "Another amazing experience awaited me! Radiation is fire. Radiation destroys. I began immediately using Reiki as a protection method, in addition to its healing energies, to transmute the fire of the radiation." At the same time, a team of Reiki practitioners, with skills in absentee healing, sent healing energies to her twice a day.

The radiation treatments severely burned her throat. She could not eat, she rapidly lost forty-five pounds, and she lost enormous amounts of energy daily. As she later wrote, "And this was with Reiki! I can't imagine what it would have been like without it [Reiki]. All I can judge by are the comments of the nurses and doctors made during my treatments and afterwards, and seeing other patients having similar treatment. They were worse off than I. At one point, I was told that very few people can complete the treatments without a break. I did. Thank God for Reiki!"

Before the next surgery, she came to the Reiki Center in Atlanta for nine days. Several of us devoted many hours day and night to giving her long Reiki treatments. She wrote later, "They were so caring, so loving, so kind and helpful. . . . I went home uplifted and confident. They helped me to survive."

The final surgery was successful—the tumor had been totally encapsulated without spreading. In the hospital, she gave herself Reiki treatments and could feel the vital energy being restored into her depleted being. In addition, a close friend, who had also studied Reiki, gave her daily treatments in the hospital. The doctors and nurses were surprised at the rate of her recovery, and she was released ahead of schedule.

In telephone conversations with my friend, the wholistic medical doctor, he warned that for full recovery she would need to change many old patterns, be more aware of nutrition, and "do *lots* of Reiki!" The name of the game for cancer patients is restoring and conserving *energy*.

One year later I saw her again. The healing and wholing process was wonderfully evident. She had continued doing a great deal of Reiki *and* had managed to change some old, limiting, unhealthy patterns. She and her husband had even moved to another state! Recently, she wrote to me about her experiences. She had used several approaches to healing and feels that they all have "their place in the universe." She had realized that "Reiki touches every level and works in conjunction with all approaches—assisting, enhancing and perfecting the energies of each of them." At her last visit to her surgeon, late in 1981, he expressed surprise and pleasure at her appearance and good health. As far as he could tell by examination, she is free of the cancer. There is nearly no evidence of the surgery—almost no scarring is visible on her neck. Because of the skill and expertise of the surgeon and the light-energy of Reiki restoring and balancing vital energy, she is on a new cycle of growth and transformation. She feels that she would "not be alive, well and whole today" if she had not had Reiki.

What causes cancer? Why do some people get cancer while others do not? "Why me? What did I do wrong?" No one has simple, easy answers to these questions. Medical researchers continue to seek causes and solutions. Modern medical technology continues to offer treatments in line with the extent of its current but limited knowledge.

Cancer research suggests that cancer has many causes that could combine to result in the malignant cells. Carcinogenic substances, genetic predisposition, polluted air, water, and food supplies, radiation, and emotion-mental factors have all been related to cancer. Scientific researchers, however, have difficulty concluding unequivocally that any one of these factors is the only cause of cancer.

Regardless of the controversy, scientific research, and speculation about the causes of cancer, the person who is *experiencing* this illness must find ways of treating and dealing with it. From a wholistic perspective, a person can combine several therapies to promote the healing process and can become a responsible participant in this process. Perhaps the most significant benefit of Reiki to cancer patients is in the simple, direct, easy-to-learn method, which allows the person to participate in restoring health. When faced with serious illnesses, a person often feels helpless and powerless. Reiki gives the opportunity for an individual to become directly involved in the healing process. Reiki helps to minimize or eliminate completely this sense of helplessness or powerlessness. With Reiki, self-confidence is restored.

In the cases discussed in this section, one significant point was that each of those persons, at some point in dealing with illness, *decided* to become actively involved in the life process that was happening to him or her.

Medical therapies were successfully combined with the Reiki

technique. The benefits of Reiki were especially noted in restoring depleted vital energy, enhancing the other therapies, and releasing emotional-mental stress. Death is not a disease, and, in the case of the person who went through the dying process, Reiki provided a vital source of confidence, inner strength, new insights, and peace of mind.

Pets, Plants, and Reiki

*All living things—both plant and animal
—are linked in an extraordinarily designed, ecological balance. Man has an
essential role to play in this chain of
regeneration.*

R. Buckminster Fuller

Reiki is vital life energy and therefore can be used effectively
on anything that is *alive!* Animals and plants are an integral part
of our planetary system, and their destiny is linked with ours.
Certain species of animals and plants are becoming extinct because mankind in modern societies has forgotten his *connection*
with other living creatures. In our journey toward wholeness in
this New Age, we will all have to learn to share this planet with
the native animals and plants who not only have the right to
be here but also are a vital, integral part of our entire ecological
system. Animals and plants exhibit an awareness different from
ours, yet they share with us intelligence, natural growth cycles,
health, disease, and death. Different does not mean inferior!

In the area of health and disease, animals and plants are
affected as are human beings by the ravages of polluted air,
water, and food sources. Because of their close contact with
humans, domesticated pets share to an even greater degree the

maladies currently arising in contemporary life. In recent times, pets have increasingly incurred diseases similar to ours. Motorized vehicles are constant sources of accidents and death for our pets. Pet psychologists have appeared on the scene to help when pets display emotional disorders from close contact with distressed human beings. Recently, *Time* magazine did an article on the use of massage therapy for pets suffering from physical stress caused by the pressures and rigors of modern life. *New Age* magazine featured a story on chiropractic techniques for animals. Of all the books available on wholistic health and natural healing, almost none offer a separate chapter on animals and pets. This book does. Reiki is vital light-energy, and the Reiki technique can be used successfully on your pets and plants. Let me share a few of the many experiences I have on record of using Reiki to help pets, nondomesticated animals, and plants.

A Reiki therapist in Atlanta received a call from a local veterinarian to assist him with his own dog. His four-year-old female Great Dane had jumped a barbed-wire fence, missed, and mutilated the entire undersection of her body. He had operated on his dog twice in an attempt to get the skin and wounds to heal but to no avail. He was attempting one more operation to remove the massive amounts of dead skin. At this point, a therapist from the Reiki Center in Atlanta began giving the dog daily treatments before and after the surgery in a series of five treatments averaging thirty to forty-five minutes each. Within this small amount of time, the Great Dane healed beautifully. The veterinarian was grateful for Reiki and believed it had saved his dog's life.

A five-year old male Schnauzner named Erich, belonging to a friend of mine, suddenly contracted the devasting parvo disease. His owner had been gone all day and had returned home late in the evening. She noticed the dog was listless and not hungry. A couple of hours later, she discovered large amounts of dried blood that he had vomited. Realizing that he was severely ill, she took his temperature and found it was nearly 106 degrees. He was extremely dehydrated from diarrhea, and his body was ice cold. She rushed him to the veterinarian at 11:30 P.M. In the car, a friend gave Erich Reiki all the way to the office, and his icy skin became lukewarm. The doctor gave the dog an appropriate injection but told my friend that it was doubtful the dog would survive the night.

After returning home, she called several people who were trained in Second Degree Reiki, which includes a highly efficient absentee-healing method. They agreed to help by sending Erich healing energy. By the next morning the dog had improved but still was not "out of the woods." Another friend, trained in Reiki, volunteered to go to the clinic and to administer complete Reiki treatments on Erich. The veterinarian was open to any help offered. In just two days, the dog had almost totally recovered and, to the amazement of all, including his doctor, Erich was eating normally and regaining energy and strength. To verify the disease, a blood test was taken. The test showed a positive reading—it was parvo. The dog had made a remarkable recovery in an unheard-of short time from a perilous, frequently fatal disease.

Erich's Reiki treatments continued on a daily basis, sometimes twice a day, to restore his energy level and eliminate all the effects of the devastating disease. Reiki literally had saved his life. It is important to note that the dog had been receiving Reiki treatments from its owner for nearly three years before this episode. During these years, she had found Reiki to be an extremely effective preventive technique for all her pets, including two cats. Her vet bills were low, and her pets were maintaining high levels of positive health. When parvo hit her dog, his preexisting positive health level and life-energy reservoir from the Reiki treatments diminished the overall impact.

Now for the dramatic story of Buckwheat, who has become known as the "miracle dog of Atlanta," as told by his owner in edited form. Late one evening in June, eight-year-old Buckwheat sat on the patio watching over his backyard domain. He had shared a late-night piece of cake with his owners. Suddenly, two large dogs jumped the fence and attacked the friendly, easygoing hound dog. In the ensuing battle, his neck was nearly broken, his ears torn, his throat bitten, and he suffered severe liver damage. When his owners found him, he was in shock, dazed, disoriented, and near death. The veterinarian did all that he could, but Buckwheat did not respond well. He was losing vitality daily.

In July, a friend who had taken Reiki came to see him. Lynn knew immediately that he needed more help than the medication and nursing care were providing. She gave Reiki treatment to Buckwheat for an hour.

Days went by, and Buckwheat continued to get worse. His muscles were degenerating, the saliva glands were not functioning, and his weight dropped from thirty to fifteen pounds. The veterinarian concluded that his liver was damaged beyond repair and, regretfully, recommended that the dog be put to sleep. Lynn was informed of the situation and thereupon began a series of intensive Reiki treatments on Buckwheat. In addition, when she went home at night she used the Reiki absentee-healing method on him. Lynn felt that, through Reiki, she was able to feel intuitively the dog's vital energy level as well as his will to live.

With all the Reiki treatments he was receiving, his energy level increased, he regained use of his neck, ate well, and actually barked—the healing process had begun. It was "uphill" from that moment on. Now that he could finally eat, his diet was enriched with whole grains, fresh vegetables, meat, and eggs and always more Reiki! Several weeks later the vet examined him again and could not believe it was the same dog—even Buckwheat's liver *appeared to have regenerated itself*. The vet actually thought he was another hound dog. But the scars and torn ears, though healed now, validated Buckwheat's miraculous recovery.

I have not yet had the honor of meeting Buckwheat, but his gracious owner took the next Reiki class with me for Buckwheat, for herself, and for her husband. She told the class of Buckwheat's "Reiki tale" and assured us that "his upset emotions and trauma had disappeared and that he had completely recovered his sense of humor, his playfulness, charm, and friendliness." With Reiki, Buckwheat has been restored to health, to wholeness, and to life.

Many people who have taken the Reiki course have reported how effective Reiki has been in treating a wide variety of disorders of dogs and other pets. One man found Reiki helpful in getting his German Shepherd through her epileptic attacks. One woman's sixteen-year-old poodle had been suffering from severe coughing attacks and excessive liquids in the lungs. She used Reiki each day on her dog and, within a week, these symptoms had reduced significantly. One woman reported that she used the Reiki on her dog's head every day for only ten minutes, and his highly tense, volatile energy changed to normal. In a Reiki class, one woman called Reiki a "pet lifesaver" in stopping bleeding. Hit by a car and badly bleeding from a leg wound, her dog lay dying in the street. She ran out and used Reiki, which immediately stopped the bleeding. With the help of friends, she got him to the vet, who expressed amazement at what Reiki had done. He affirmed that without Reiki the dog would have bled to death before she could get him to help.

It has been my experience as well as that of many others that cats respond well to Reiki. They seem to be able to "tune in" naturally and with ease to this life energy. I am a fond lover of cats. For twenty years I have always had at least two cats, sometimes as many as five, as regular members of my household. In addition, several others are always passing through. For years I have consistently given my cats Reiki treatments. I have found that overall they are healthier, brighter, and less frequently sick. My vet bills are lower. When the cats have needed medical treatment, it has tended to be less costly, the recovery has been quicker, and the side effects have been lessened.

I had an interesting experience with a stray who took up residence at my front door until I admitted her into the family and named her Buffy. As it turned out, Buffy had cancer of the bladder in its advanced stage. But the Reiki I did on her helped her relax and seemed to help the pain. The side effects of the medications were so potent that after consulting with the vet, I finally took her off the high doses and relied solely on Reiki. Buffy was a very lovely cat but a very sick one. Yet, with Reiki, she was able to eat and maintain her weight. When additional internal complications arose, she made her transition. She had, however, given me the opportunity of sharing her inner light and of learning how to treat sick animals with Reiki.

In Atlanta, I have done a considerable amount of healing work with cats. As a result, the Reiki Center there frequently gets calls for help with cats, and one of the diseases we treat is feline leukemia. It is a devastating disease that strikes a cat suddenly, draining it of its vital energy and almost certainly resulting in death. Because it is a highly contagious disease, the ill cat is treated in its home. Special precautions are taken with cleaning my skin and clothes to avoid spreading it to other cats as well as to my own when I return home.

Several years ago, I received a call from a dejected, extremely upset, and deeply saddened owner of a wonderful three-year-old Siamese cat named Sylvia. Misidentified as to gender early in kittenhood, Sylvia actually was a boy! He had severe feline leukemia and had been sent home by the vet with the gloomy prognosis that death could be expected shortly. His despondent owner had decided to seek additional help.

When I began doing Reiki treatments on Sylvia, he was completely lacking in vital energy. He was near death and could barely eat, and his eyes were glazed over—he was in the dying process. I gave Sylvia Reiki treatments nearly every day for the first few weeks. On the third day, he was perched in the window at my "usual" arrival time. With Reiki, the connection between us had been easily opened. Thereafter, his owner reported that he always knew when I was coming and would wait in the window for my car.

When I began the Reiki treatments with Sylvia, there were places on his body where his fur had fallen off, and he had large bluish-colored sores on his head, neck, and shoulders. During the early part of the Reiki process, his condition appeared to get much worse. He could barely move, he was extremely de-hydrated, the sores got bigger and bluer, and he lost more fur and much weight. In the natural healing process, diseases sometimes get worse before reversing. Reiki promotes this *natural* process but often reverses the disease sooner and then restores the health.

His owner was distraught at how horrible Sylvia looked. She kept checking with the vet, who reassured her that Sylvia could not be harmed and reminded her that his illness was terminal. I had added Sylvia's name to my absentee-healing list. As is my custom, I send healing to everyone on the list, people and pets, each evening. I also asked Sylvia's owner to play a certain record for him several times each day. I always take a wholistic approach to healing. With Reiki as the primary, direct source of light, life energy, I sometimes use secondary sources—especially certain musical pieces.

The process we went through with Sylvia taught me many things that later opened dimensions of understanding in my healing work with others. One evening while I was sending healing using the Second Degree Reiki, I had the experience of becoming *one* with Sylvia. It was as though I was inside him. I could see and *feel* the disease. I could clearly see the Reiki light-energy inside that cat, and I could see it as fire burning the disease *out* of him. That insight helped explain the horrible blue sores and all the draining pus. Outwardly, Sylvia was a terrible mess of sores, pus, skin, and bones. Inwardly, he was being transformed. I could also see that the negative was being *transmuted* into positive energy—it was pure, white light.

It was an incredible process to behold. I was deeply grateful for the opportunity to go through this experience with Sylvia. Since then, many people who have studied Reiki have shared similar experiences with me. With Reiki, you become a direct channel for healing light-energy. The one receiving this energy is free to use it as needed. With Reiki, you are the channel, the giver, the co-worker in the process but not the controller.

I worked with Sylvia for more than two months, sometimes daily, sometimes with absentee healing only. About midway in this process, he appeared to be ready to die at any moment. Then, suddenly, he accepted food, a light returned to his eyes, and, gradually, he began to regain strength and vital energy. He needed all the Reiki he could get! At that time, I was not a Reiki Master and therefore could not teach this technique to Sylvia's owner. But I knew deep inside of my being that I would one day become a Reiki teacher so that I could teach those close to a pet or loved one, family or friend, how to give Reiki treatments.

Meanwhile, Sylvia's vitality was restored completely. The laboratory reports indicated that the leukemia was no longer present. His new fur was thick, shiny, and beautiful. One day in early fall, I stopped by to give him another Reiki treatment. I knew when I saw this healthy, playful, very much *alive* Siamese cat that he would not need any more treatments from me. In his own special way, Sylvia let me know that day that he was completely well. Usually, when I began his Reiki treatment, he would settle down and quietly let me proceed. That day, however, with twinkling eyes, he playfully chewed my fingers, rolled around, and brought me his toys to play "fetch." With loving energy, Sylvia had dismissed me. It was my last visit with him, but occasionally through the months his grateful owner called to let me know that Sylvia was fine!

People from all parts of the country have shared with me their experiences with Reiki and cats. After receiving only the first of the Reiki transmissions, one woman reported to the class that she had gone home and "Reiki-ed" her cat, who had been listless and not eating. Within minutes, while she was administering Reiki, her cat threw up a strange-looking substance, then ate her dinner, drank some water, and returned to normal. I instructed her to continue Reiki with her cat for several days to balance her energy and restore *ki* to a normal level. She did, with positive results.

One man reported that his six-year-old cat had suffered a broken leg in an unusual fall. The leg, though set properly by the vet, was not healing as it should have. I recommended that he give the cat thirty minutes of Reiki each day, which he did. Within five days, the improvement was so enormous that the cat was going outside dragging its cast and leg. Previously, he had stayed in a corner, listless and depressed.

A woman in Minnesota said that she had taken in a stray cat who had been severely mistreated and then deserted by her owners. The cat had suffered severe emotional damage. She was afraid of people but had become aggressive rather than passive in her behavior. She would attack and bite people— even guests who came into her new owner's home. This hostile behavior continued for several years. Then her owner took the Reiki class, both First and Second Degree. She then gave Reiki to her cat on a regular basis for several months. When at work during the day, she was able to send her Reiki absentee-healing energy. Within four months, the improvement in the cat's personality was noticed by all who knew her. She began relating to people without the old fears, and her owner's friends could pet her without incurring scratches and bites. Reiki had touched the nonphysical level of her cat-being that had been bruised and battered. Her owner has kept me updated on her cat's continued progress. She reports that the cat "seems to enjoy life more now. She is less tense and now hardly ever exhibits her old, 'spooky,' jumpy, scared self." With Reiki, her healing is in progress, and she is gaining wholeness in her cat-life experience.

Sometimes in our lives, each of us might have the opportunity to help animals other than our pets. In each of the cases I am about to describe the opportunity came to me unexpectedly. I was thankful to have the gift of Reiki and to learn more about the animal kingdom that exists all around us.

I had attended a soccer game in Tampa, Florida, and had been impressed by the vigor of the Rowdies, by the incredible spirit of the crowd, and by the joyful array of colors filling the stadium. Upon leaving the game, we were sitting in the midst of a traffic jam when off to my right I saw something move in the grass near the curb. Since traffic was stopped, I got out and carefully approached what turned out to be a seagull, no doubt one of Jonathan Livingston's relatives, with a badly broken wing. It appeared that the bird had been hit by a car and abandoned. Having had no previous experience with injured, undomesticated animals, I stood there for a moment wondering what to do. The seagull could not be left there. He could not fly, he could no longer fend for himself, and he would not survive. Remembering how effective I had found Reiki to be in calming people, I took a deep breath, stepped forward, and reached out for the seagull with my Reiki hands. He fluttered and stumbled a few feet. I stopped—he stopped. I proceeded toward him again, picked him up, and got into the car. Immediately, I could feel the Reiki energy pouring from my hands into his entire body. I have always loved seagulls but had never touched one and had never held one in my hands. I could hardly believe this was happening. It was an incredible experience. Without Reiki, I know that I would not have had the confidence to touch that seagull.

With the Reiki approach, he calmed down and absorbed the vital energy being channeled into him. The seagull seemed, somehow, to know what the Reiki energy was—he seemed to know instinctively that it was healing, life-force energy. He seemed to absorb it with his whole being. I was vividly aware that the energy flowing through that seagull was the same energy flowing through me. The contact was there. He never once tried to bite me even though I did not have his beak covered. We drove from Tampa straight to the Suncoast Seabird Sanctuary in Indian Rocks Beach on the Gulf, north of St. Petersburg, Florida.

It was after midnight, dark, and cold but, after we had rung the bell several times, a sleepy but kind, gentle, elderly man admitted the seagull for treatment. I went to visit him the next morning. He was doing remarkably well after surgery. He had lost a wing, but he could still live a useful seagull-life, taking care of himself and doing his part in the ecological system. I had learned a new dimension of Reiki and, through it, had learned a great deal about the expression of the life-force energy on this planet.

About a year later, while I was walking along the seashore, I came upon a cormorant twisting around dizzily in the sand. I called to a friend for help. With both sets of Reiki hands, we managed to get the bird calmed. We used a towel over his long, active beak to avoid bites. Holding the cormorant in my lap, I began giving Reiki to this beautiful aquatic creature of nature. We went straight to the Suncoast Seabird Sanctuary, where it was determined that the cormorant had been a victim of poisoning, probably from polluted water or food. This cormorant could, however, be saved with antibiotics. We both continued doing Reiki absentee healing on this bird until it was released from the sanctuary.

Not long ago, I came across another lovely cormorant on the beach who was also in trouble. Somehow the bird's left leg had been so badly broken that it could not fly or move very far. Realizing that the bird was too alert for me to handle without proper equipment, two of us trained in Reiki began sending him absentee healing. We could only get within a couple of feet of him. Once again, I drove to the Suncoast Seabird Sanctuary for help. Earlier that day, staff from that sanctuary had tried to catch this cormorant but the bird had gotten into the water and avoided the net. With the Reiki light-energy in contact with the bird, I knew he was ready to be helped.

Reiki had provided a direct connection of healing energy, letting him know that it was safe to accept help. He was calmer and more trusting now. This time, a friend and I did Reiki without touching the bird physically, and he was captured and treated. His leg is healing now, and he will soon be free. Reiki was an essential tool for use in helping this beautiful but severely injured bird. Without such an effective technique, I might have been just another person passing by the bird, sympathetic to its plight but not knowing what to do.

Modern scientific research has given us much information about plant sensitivity and plant awareness. Caring for household and garden plants is a rewarding though serious endeavor. We have evidence that plants respond to our love and caring attention and that they shrink from attacks by people and pets. Being life, light-energy, Reiki is a highly effective tool for use in working with plants.

One woman shared her exciting experience with growing a summer vegetable garden and using Reiki. She reported, "I held each seed in my hands pouring Reiki into them. I seemed to be able to sense the life-force energy within the seeds in connection with the Reiki coming from my hands. When the seeds began sprouting, I would carefully cup my hands around the small plants giving several minutes of Reiki to each. In the process of 'Reiking' my vegetables several times a week, I myself experienced a deep sense of inner peace. I felt as though I had been one with the natural growth cycle. I was much less tense and more centered than I had ever been in my life. I was also doing a Reiki treatment on myself early each morning. The beautiful, full, large vegetables my family and I ate all summer were the reward of my efforts. My friends and family were amazed at my gardening success that summer in contrast to my previous failures. There is simply no doubt in my mind that Reiki was the ingredient responsible for such abundance."

Now for the famous rubber plant story of Atlanta. During the second session of a Reiki Seminar, a woman brought in a pathetic, nearly dead rubber plant. She had gotten it for twenty-eight cents at a local K-Mart. With barely a spark of life in it, the little plant was green-brown and sagging in its pot. In the previous class, I had discussed the use of Reiki with all living things, including plants. But I will have to admit that when I saw her bringing in that more than half-dead plant, I myself had a moment of hesitation. I took a deep breath, continued the seminar, and "Reiki-ed" that plant for all I was worth.

Others in the class helped give it Reiki from its roots up, which is the best place to begin. The vital Reiki energy can then be carried upward and distributed. Several months later I had occasion to talk with this woman and, tentatively, I asked her about the plant. With enthusiasm, she responded that it had grown incredibly! She had taken it to her office, and sometimes she put it under her desk to give it Reiki between her feet all day. Everyone in the office had watched in amazement as it got bigger and bigger. Pieces had been cut, and additional offspring of this gigantic plant had been given away. The story of this once nearly dead rubber plant with its Reiki healing became widely known. There is no doubt that with Reiki this plant had progressed in its natural evolution to wholeness and, in the process, its story had touched all of us deeply.

Many people have reported similar experiences with Reiki and their plants. One man wrote of his success in growing roses with Reiki; another told of the healing and reenergizing of his favorite willow tree. A woman in Florida shared her experience of using the Reiki absentee-healing method on her delicate flower bushes and citrus trees during the hard freeze in 1980. By spring, her yard was in full array, lush with budding life. Her neighbors, who had lost their plants, were amazed at the abundance of her yard. Hers was the only living, green back-yard on the block!

The purpose of this chapter has been to share experiences about how effective Reiki has been with pets, other animals, and plants. There are many additional ways Reiki could be used in this context. One of the unique aspects of Reiki is that it provides a connection for vital light-energy, which can be used creatively and efficiently and adapted to any situation by the person with the Reiki touch. Someday I hope to see Reiki in the hands of everyone who owns pets and plants and of all professionals who deal daily with the magnificent pets, other animals, and plants of our world.

13

Death, Dying, and Reiki

> *Right up until the moment of transition one carries all the results of existence in space and time within the essence and the self. But at transformation, all of that will be left behind. One enters the new life without remnants of the past.*
>
> **Sufi, Al Wasi**

One of the most important, significant, and profound things you will ever do in this life is die. In fact, taken from an expanded perspective, the two major events of your life are your birth and death. Your birth marked a dramatic transition from a previous energy state, whatever the form, into a "life" on what we perceive as the physical plane. Just as profoundly, your death is a process of making a transition from this physical form to that of another level of being. There is no proof that consciousness is terminated at one's physical death on this plane. In fact, quite the contrary appears to be true!

Throughout our history on this planet, since we first contemplated the extent and depth of our being, we have always spoken and written of a reality existing beyond the limits of this so-called physical plane. In modern times, the Swiss psychiatrist

96

Carl Jung said, "Nobody can say where man ends."[1] His statement reflects ancient man's assertion that there is a continuum of life and consciousness even though the outer forms change.

More than five thousand years ago, the Egyptians affirmed their knowledge of the immortality of human consciousness. In *The Book of the Dead,* which the Egyptians actually called the *Book of Coming Forth to Light,* many levels of the life of the soul were described, and it was written, "I am like the stars who know not weariness—I am upon the Boat of Millions of Years."[2] The inner knowledge about life and science was kept secret and hidden, revealed to only a few chosen initiates. But in the current New Age of humanity, the doors are being thrown open and the knowledge distributed to all of us.

Attributed to Lao Tsu is the statement, "There is a reality prior to heaven and earth."[3] Plato wrote, "The body of heaven is visible, but the soul is invisible, and partakes of reason and harmony."[4] In the Middle Ages, St. Thomas Aquinas stated, "The soul exists independent of the body, and continues after the body dies, taking up a new spiritual body."[5] In the new physics, consciousness is associated with all the quantum mechanical processes. Eugene Wigner, American Nobel Prize winner, puts it this way, "The recognition that physical objects and spiritual values have a very similar kind of reality has contributed to my mental peace. It is the only known point of view which is consistent with quantum mechanics."[6] Sir Arthur Eddington commented, "It is a primitive form of thought that things either exist or do not exist."[7] To this rich tradition Elisabeth Kubler-Ross adds, "I am convinced that there is life after death . . . death does not really exist."[8]

In all of human history, no culture has tended to treat the dying in such an antiseptic, noninvolved manner as we do. In our society, we treat the dying as though they were actually dying rather than being in the process of a transition and a birthing into another state of being. Dying and death are an integral part of human life, setting the boundaries in which we can measure our life's meaning. Elisabeth Kubler-Ross wrote,

"But if we can learn to view death from a different perspective, to reintroduce it into our lives so that it comes not as a dreaded stranger but as an expected companion to our life, then we can learn to live our lives with meaning—with full appreciation of our finiteness, of the limits of our time here."⁹

Death is not a disease. It is one of the most significant, dramatic, and meaningful acts of your life, completing a cycle of existence on this plane. Death is not a final termination of your being. Death is a beautiful natural process of integrating all that you have been into the always present and eternal moment of "being here now." Death is the deep, full breath we take as we make our transition into the next phase of our unfolding process. In truth, it is a glorious moment of "birthing" ourselves into a new existence.

Dying and death are a process in which we are utterly and completely involved from the moment of our physical birth. In our modern society, we have been disconnected from our own source, we have been unplugged and separated from our life-sustaining line, and we have "forgotten" how to make that prime, essential contact with who we really are.

Continued attention has been given to the gains of the outer world with little regard for our inner being, and, as a group, we have fallen asleep and become unconscious to our "real connection." Dazzled by modern technologies and blinded by the sensationalism of outer forms, we have lost touch with our myths, true religion, rituals, and symbols, which carefully preserved and transmitted to us knowledge essential to our wholeness.

Somehow, dying in our culture has become not only un-speakable but also unthinkable! It is not polite. In our society today, it has become the "supreme taboo." We tend to consider dying as the "worst thing" that can possibly happen to us. Yet dying is a completely natural, fulfilling, culminating, and libera-ting experience—no matter when it comes to each of us. There is no tragic or untimely death. There is only that which is part of your total unfolding. All the pieces fit as a part of a larger whole. Indeed, no single piece could be cast aside once it has been set into motion. Without each part, the whole would not be what it is.

In my healing work with Reiki, I have had many opportunities for growth and increased understanding of the nature of healing and wholing. Needless to say, the biggest challenges and most profound opportunities came when I was called in to try to "save someone from death." Let me share one of my early opportunities to use Reiki in a terminal illness situation.

I was called by the family of a man in his early thirties who was dying of liver cancer. Having heard from a friend that I "had cured her tumor," Phil's wife and mother insisted that I was to come and perform a miracle healing. After the phone call, I went into prayer and meditation. I knew that I had not *personally* cured their friend's tumor, but rather that I, acting as a channel, had transmitted the Reiki light-energy to her. From the phone call, I was aware of the desperate, tense, and highly emotionally charged energy of Phil's wife and mother. Their demand for me "to do an instantaneous healing" left no doubt as to the degree of their expectations.

One of my most important early lessons in healing work, for which I am filled with deep gratitude, was that of letting go of ego in the healing process. The healer or the transmitter of light-energy cannot let the outer self seek its own satisfaction or gratification in any way. Nor can your ego be attached to outer results and expectations.

When I arrived at the hospital, I met Phil, who was, as it turned out, in his very last stages of life on this plane. Because of heavy drug doses, he was not conscious then, nor did he ever regain consciousness. The cancer had spread from his liver and pancreas to his lungs and stomach. Additional complications had set in because of the extreme deterioration of his bodily functions. Because of his weakened and terminal state, the doctors had determined that surgery was not possible. His wife and mother were hysterical and in shock.

What happened in the following days gave me deep knowledge of Reiki as a complete and profound technique for use in the dying and death process. Reiki is the best tool I know of for someone to use in helping, supporting, and nurturing the body, mind, and soul of oneself or of another person in the dying process. In the last days of his life, I gave Phil many complete Reiki treatments, spending extra time on his liver and pancreas. During the night after the first Reiki treatment, he discharged enormous amounts of mucus from his lungs. From then on he could breathe more normally, whereas before he was gasping, struggling to breathe, and choking on the clogged mucus in his throat and lungs. The next morning the doctor was amazed at how much the extreme swelling in Phil's liver had been diminished. Color and radiance were already being restored to Phil's gray, pale face—he was resting peacefully, but he *was* going through his dying process.

During the next five days, I continued to give Phil complete Reiki treatments. In the early hours of the sixth day, Phil released from his body. It had been a deep honor to assist him in this beautiful process. Reiki had opened a direct line inwardly from him to me. This contact was directly in touch with his soul. It was an exquisite experience—it was one of pure ecstasy—it was beyond the limits of these words. With the Reiki light-energy, Phil had received immediate benefits on the physical plane in making him more comfortable for his death. But Reiki also touched deeply into the essence of his being. I saw his Light and, silently within, I knew him, knew his struggles and his triumphs, knew his Light, was one with him, shared the entire magnificent process of dying with him, and was awed by its majesty. It changed his life, and it changed mine. The old fears, misunderstandings, and misinterpretations of death fell away, dissolved almost instantly.

The experience I had shared with him in the inner dimensions was one of joy, one of fullness, one of celebration. It was as though a cosmic event of great significance was happening and all the stars were there—the Light was incredible. In the inner being, the entire process was powerful yet gentle, yang yet yin—filled with Light. His inner peace was overwhelming.

And, in sharp contrast, the outer activities in the room around him seemed trivial, empty, and not real—the sterility of the hospital, the hesitancy of the staff, the fears and numb resignation of his mother, the mounting terror, anger, and bitterness of his wife. Everyone around him was caught up in the outer process—that of his body letting go of the life-force, the *ki*. In the outer form, it appeared to be somehow cold and final, but, *at the same time,* in the inner planes, a great event was taking place. The outer appearance was only an illusion. The truth was in the inner process, and through Reiki, I had come in conscious contact with it.

In ancient Tibet and Egypt, instructions were given to the dying person on how to release the soul from the body and how to make the profound transition from one state of being to another. Someone usually participated in the dying process, acting as a guide, a support system. Today we tend to avoid participation in the dying process. We leave the dying alone, rationalizing our fears with "let him die in private," "call me when it's over," or "she would prefer to be alone."

Reiki bridges the gap from the ancient wisdom to the modern predicament. In many situations, since my early experience with Phil and Reiki, I have worked with people in the dying process. The Reiki technique and its open line with light-energy provides the channel for contact with all levels of the person's being and provides a safe, natural technique for releasing energy from the body at death. The experience of death is no longer to be feared. Our daily lives can be lived with a new perspective, with a dynamic wholeness, and with an awareness of our own im-mortality. At the "continuum" exhibition in Minneapolis, a deeply provocative question is posed: "If you were sure of your own immortality, would you live your life differently?" The experience of death is no longer to be feared. Our daily lives can be lived with a new perspective, with a dynamic wholeness, and with an awareness of our own immortality.

In the Reiki classes, I instruct on how to use Reiki to its fullest in helping a family member, a friend, or a patient in the process of dying and death. Many people have written to me through the years expressing how the Reiki technique itself gave them the confidence to reach out and touch loved ones who were dying, how much they had learned in this process about death and ultimately about life, and how new vistas had opened about the concept of immortality.

One gentleman returned to a Reiki class to share his experience with Reiki as a death and dying technique. He gave us this account. His father was hospitalized with terminal cancer. Tom was called to come immediately because death was expected any minute. From childhood, Tom's relationship with his father had been extremely difficult. As a sensitive, artistic child, Tom had withdrawn from his father's domineering "macho" mentality. Before he was ten, Tom had been taken by his mother to another city to live. Through the years, his only contacts with his father, though sparse, had been at best unpleasant. In addition, his father's alcoholism had been a "turn-off" for Tom. Through the years, he had continued to harbor bitter resentment, hostility, and hatred for his father.

Tom was in his mid-fifties now, but, when the phone call came demanding his immediate presence at his father's deathbed, the old angers exploded inside him. Reluctantly, he left for New York. As each step took him closer to his dying father, his tensions increased to a substantial anxiety level.

Outside his father's hospital room, Tom took a deep breath, opened the door, and came face to face with this man, who had held such power over him emotionally and mentally through all these years. Here was his father, now broken, weak, pale, barely conscious, and nearly dead. The level of physical pain his father was experiencing was excruciating. He was barely able to speak to Tom.

Tom said that, in that moment, the only thing he could think of was to do Reiki. His father's pain was increased by the additional complications of severe arthritis and a difficult heart problem. He could only be given a limited amount of pain pills. His father's extreme pain had triggered compassion in Tom. He told us that had it not been for Reiki, he would have felt completely helpless, he would have been a passive bystander, and he might even have avoided staying in his father's room.

As it turned out, his father asked him repeatedly for Reiki

because it was relieving his severe pain. Remarkably, his father's color was returning and his eyes were getting brighter. Tom noted that a radiance, a "light-energy," began to emanate from his father's head almost from the first contact with Reiki.

By the end of the second day, his father was resting well, but the *ki* was vacating his physical form. Tom said they had devised a hand signal for his father to let him know when he wanted Reiki. Talking took too much energy. Around noon of the third day, his father made his transition. Tom was holding his dying father's head while doing Reiki. He then did some Reiki on his father's heart center. He told me that he could feel his own oneness with his father's essence—it was warm and peaceful, filled with love and light. He said that with Reiki he could "feel" his father's soul releasing from the physical form. Later, as Tom was leaving, he saw that the entire room was radiating with a magnificent white-light-energy.

Tom had shared his experience with the class because he wanted others to know how important Reiki had been as a dying and death technique. For once, he and his father had shared love and peace on an inner, silent, and *real* level. He said that he knew there was much left inside him about his father that needed working out, but Reiki had opened most of the doors previously sealed with negativity from the past.

There are no limits to how Reiki can be used with any person or pet experiencing the process of dying. The momentous occasion of death represents a truly cosmic happening as the soul continues on its journey into new dimensions. The Reiki technique gives you a powerful yet gentle way of participating without intruding, of touching life, not death, and of experiencing oneness, not separateness, with the one going through this profound process.

What a wonderful day it will be when nurses, doctors, and other professionals treating the dying are also trained in Reiki. What a valuable technique for others, such as the Hospice groups, who work with terminal people. Reiki can be easily incorporated into the conventional medical framework and into other, alternative methods as well. What a beautiful New Age in each of us when we use Reiki as a light-energy tool for helping, guiding, nurturing, and supporting ourselves, our loved ones, our friends, and our fellow humans and our pets through the natural process of dying.

14

Instantaneous Healing with Reiki

Energy can enter and leave space-time.

Dr. Jack Sarfatti

Throughout the history of mankind's journey on this planet, accounts of instantaneous healings are found again and again. It is true, indeed, that so far not everyone in every situation experiences instantaneous healing, but this phenomenon does exist not as a possibility but as a fact of human experience. As Eugene Wigner, American Nobel Prize winner, put it, "Every phenomenon is unexpected and most unlikely until it has been discovered. And some of them remain unreasonable for a long time after they have been discovered."[1]

What is instantaneous healing and what are some of the aspects of the mechanism involved? The dictionary defines *instantaneous* as "occurring or completed without delay."[2] A related word is *spontaneous,* which is defined as "happening or arising without apparent external cause; self-generated; voluntary and impulsive; unpremeditated."[3] In Reiki Seminars, I generally employ the term "spontaneous healings" in reference to experiences in which healing or wholing occurs within a relatively short period of time with the use of Reiki. Some people have also had instantaneous healings with Reiki.

The essential mechanism underneath a spontaneous healing

105

can be understood in the term "extempore" from the Latin *ex* meaning "out of" and *tempus* meaning "time." Spontaneous healings occur in that space which transcends the limits of the outer world and the outer self—the body, emotions, and mind. The person is *literally* "out of time" during this process. The person experiencing spontaneous healing is liberated for an instant, freed in a flash, released from the bondage of old patterns, and connected directly with the eternal, universal life-force. There are no limits in that dimension.

Descriptions of instantaneous healings by people who have had the experience include several elements of similarity. For example, descriptions include seeing or becoming intense, pure "white light," having no sense of time as we know it, oneness with God, freedom from fear, and transcending to a total awareness. This experience takes the individual out of the old patterns or limits and shifts him into another dimension of being. Sometimes such an experience occurs when one is in deep meditation or through creative imagery and even in moments of intense crisis. With Reiki, spontaneous healing can happen with direct use and focusing of this light-energy.

One of my clients who was bringing her eleven-year-old daughter for Reiki treatments for eczema arrived late for a session. She and her daughter were visibly upset, and the three-month-old baby was still crying. As they were on their way to my office, a car had stopped suddenly in front of their car, and the baby had been hurled off the front seat, had banged his forehead on the dashboard, and had fallen to the floor. The bump on his head was severely swollen, bright red, and, from his yells, still painful. We all sat down, and I held the baby, putting my Reiki hands on the bump. We all talked, and everyone began to relax. Immediately the baby stopped crying, and within four minutes of doing Reiki the swelling and the redness on his head had disappeared. His mother and sister were truly astonished. I suggested that they both take the Reiki Seminar so that in the future *they* could use Reiki in emergency situations as well as other times.

A nurse in Detroit, who had taken Reiki, works in an elementary school. A young girl stung by a bee was brought screaming into her office. The child's arm was swollen, red, and stinging. The nurse sat her down in a chair and began doing Reiki on the arm while talking to the child. The nurse reported that within minutes the bee's stinger fell out of the wound, the swelling left, and the redness was gone. In addition, the child's usually allergic reactions to bee stings never happened. Both she and the child were amazed at this instantaneous healing with Reiki. In a few more minutes, the little girl was dismissed and resumed her outdoor play.

Susan and her date were leaving a London theater. It was a rainy, cold night in January. Suddenly she slipped down the stairs, hitting her knees with great force, tumbled across the sidewalk, and bumped into a street lamp. The pain in both her knees and in her head was excruciating. In a blurry moment, she remembered to do Reiki. She sat there doing Reiki for a few minutes until the pain and swelling in her knees and head subsided. Then she got up, and the two went on with their evening. She said that without Reiki not only would she have been hurt for a longer time but also that her entire vacation in England would have been destroyed. She had no doubt about the severity of the injuries and the effectiveness of Reiki "on the spot."

An attorney, Ken, who took the Reiki class to help a beloved niece through the terminal phase of a very difficult disease, reported during the second class session that his four-year-old son had fallen down the stairs to the backyard. He had heard the scream and dashed immediately to help the boy. The child had a large bump on his head and was crying uncontrollably. Ken held the child and did Reiki on the bruise and on the back of his head. Within minutes, the bump and bruise were gone and the boy was completely calm and went on to play. Ken noted that this experience was amazing for two main reasons: (1) the complete healing of the bump with Reiki in just a few minutes and (2) the child's change to calmness. Ken said that his son had always been particularly frightened of any falls, large or small, and it usually took several hours to calm him down after such an experience. Ken had four other children and said he was glad to have Reiki for future use and to save on medical bills!

One woman wrote that when she was cleaning a crystal chandelier, a 75-watt bulb, which had been burning for about five hours, touched her right upper arm. She realized it was burning but could not jump quickly because she was involved with replacing a heavy strand of crystal. She finally moved slowly off the chair and did Reiki for only ten minutes. She said that "the deep crescent-shaped burn on her upper arm was gone—the spot never blistered, peeled, hurt, or discolored."

A woman in New York, who was in her sixties and was using Reiki successfully to treat a severe, eighteen-year-old arthritis condition, wrote about her other Reiki benefits. One cold, windy, snowy morning, she had gotten up with the beginnings of a sinus cold. She wrote that "one ten-minute Reiki treatment and my sinuses were *normal*." She added at the end of the letter that the fee for the Reiki Seminar was "a drop in the bucket, as they say—what you are teaching is priceless!"

A woman in her early thirties was scheduled for surgery on a large kidney stone that would not dissolve with medication. Carol and Larry, business associates of hers, gave her a forty-five minute Reiki treatment and suggested that she have X-rays before surgery because Reiki could dissolve internal stones. The next day she checked into the hospital and, after much difficulty, managed to get additional X-rays. To everyone's surprise, to the doctor's chagrin, and to her own relief, the kidney stone was gone. Her surgery was canceled. After a year, she reported no recurrence of the condition.

Twenty-three-year-old Jim worked as a welder in a sheet metal factory. His mother had given him the Reiki class as a special Christmas gift. After the second Reiki session, he went to work. At the job, he reached for a piece of hot metal, picked it up, and realized he had on only one of his special gloves—his other hand was bare. Immediately, he felt pain. He dropped the hot metal, sat down, and did Reiki on his

hand. He said he was afraid to move or to look at his hand—
he just sat, bent over, doing Reiki. About thirty minutes later,
he looked at his hand. The healing had been spontaneous. There
was no swelling, no redness, no pain, and no blisters. The dirt that
had been on his fingers was now clearly embedded in his skin.
The skin on his hand was smooth and shiny as though it had
been ironed. Everyone in the class examined his hand and
realized that Reiki had promoted an instantaneous healing. He
said he did not know what he would have done without Reiki.
Later, his boss confirmed that the temperature on the metal at
the time he moved it would have been 1,200 to 1,500 degrees—
impossible to touch with a bare hand without severe, permanent
damage.

On a tour of Egypt in 1980, sponsored by the American
International Reiki Association, one of the women tripped on a
large cement block and fell heavily. She had not seen the block
and did not have time to buffer the fall. She hit hard on the
base of her tailbone. She said the immediate pain was excruciating and she lost consciousness. I was standing a few feet
away, saw the accident, ran to her, and did Reiki on the base
of her spine and the top of her head. Instantaneously, she
regained consciousness, the pain dissolved, she stood up, and
her recovery was complete. She said, "When you touched me
I could see, somewhere in my being, the white-light energy of
Reiki going up my spine. I could feel my legs, back, and head
being healed instantly." The entire process from her fall to her
spontaneous healing took less than one minute.

A woman reported that her husband had come home badly
frightened and with a neck injury from a car accident. Realizing
that he was in a state of anxiety and shock, she stretched him
out on the floor and gave him a Reiki treatment while he
continued explaining what had happened. Instantly, the pain and
swelling left his neck and, within ten minutes, he had completely
relaxed. Reiki had spontaneously balanced his energies emotionally and physically.

During a Reiki class, I was demonstrating the special
treatment positions on a man in his late forties. While I was

talking, I had kept my hand on the upper part of his spine. All of a sudden, we all heard a loud "pop." Surprised, I stopped in mid-sentence. The man I was using for demonstration said he had been healed instantly of a painful blocked energy spot where a vertebra had been out of place for several months and had resisted healing with other therapies. With Reiki, there is no need to manipulate body parts—the light-energy had been enough to snap it back into place!

I was exiting an auditorium through two very large and very heavy wooden doors and caught a finger between the two doors as they closed shut with force! The pain was intense. The finger turned bright red and swelled immediately. I sat down outside and did Reiki on it for fifteen minutes. The pain stopped instantaneously. When I looked at my finger, its color and size had returned to normal. I was amazed. Reiki had spontaneously reversed the injury process! There was no trace of any damage to the finger.

On the third day of a Reiki class, a young mother, Karen, came into the room with obvious joy! She had been unsure of Reiki but had taken it to use for herself in healing some difficult health problems. Karen told us her story. Her two young children had been wrestling in the living room and one accidentally tossed the other, who bumped his head on the corner of the TV. A large red bump swelled up across his entire forehead. Everyone panicked. His grandfather ran to get ice, his grandmother ran to get a wet cloth, and Karen immediately put her Reiki hands on his forehead amid his loud screaming. Instantly, the bump was gone. By then, the others had returned with all the various remedies. The little boy was laughing. They were all sold on Reiki as they saw for themselves that there was no trace whatever of the previously severe bruise— no swelling, no redness, and no discoloration. Her son said, "Mommy, now you have magic hands!"

This boy's words reminded me of Arthur C. Clarke's famous "Third Law," which states, "Any sufficiently advanced technology is indistinguishable from magic." This idea reflects the process involved with Reiki.

Many people frequently report to me instantaneous healings during one of the four Reiki activating energy transmissions given in the seminar. The descriptions are usually similar to one another. A woman in her fifties, who had been a psychic healer for twenty years, reported an instantaneous healing of a severe lower back injury during one of the Reiki transmissions. During this process, she said she felt intense warmth, saw "white light," and felt the blocked energy release from her back. After twelve years, this injury was still causing severe pain and restricting her daily activities. Now she was free of it. When I saw her a year later, she confirmed that the spontaneous healing had been complete and that with daily use of Reiki she was feeling better than ever as well as looking young and radiant.

During the first Reiki activating transmission, Marilyn reported to the class that she felt her neck being healed instantaneously with an intensely warm energy. Three years previously she had been in a car accident that had severely injured her neck. She had tried various therapies, but nothing had released the pain and stiffness. During the next Reiki sessions, Marilyn was thrilled to show everyone how easily she could now turn her head from side to side.

Robert, a young man in his late twenties from Chicago, returned to one of my lectures two years after taking the Reiki Seminar. He told the audience that, during the fourth activating transmission, he had experienced an emotional, instantaneous healing. He had been too shy to say anything to me. He also wanted to be sure it would last. He explained that he had seen a flash of white light, had felt hot and cold at the same time, and had experienced a release of anger, anxiety, and fear that he had been storing for years. He knew that he had been healed emotionally. He also knew that he was now free of his extreme addiction to cigarettes. In the subsequent two years, he had never smoked again.

A man in his early fifties noticed that a chronically stiff shoulder healed spontaneously during a Reiki transmission. He reported to the class that he saw a flash of white light, felt a deep warmth, and felt the energy in his shoulder revitalize instantly.

A woman suffering for several years with chronic pain and stiffness in the back of her neck was healed spontaneously during the third Reiki activating energy. She told the class that she saw a deep purple color, then white light, felt enormous heat, then immense peace and a lifting away of the negative energy in her neck.

These examples reflect just a few of the many instances in which spontaneous healing or wholing has happened with Reiki. Reiki acts as a catalyst to trigger quantum leaps as described in new physics. In instantaneous healing a sudden transformation happens rather than a gradual change—a shift is made to direct contact with energy at a higher order. The old patterns and limits are transcended, and a new dimension is tapped.

15

The Gift of Reiki:
A New Beginning

Here is a test to find whether your mission on earth is finished: if you're alive, it isn't.

Richard Bach

A New Age is happening for all of humanity and simultaneously a "new age" is breaking for many of us from within ourselves. Advancing into the "new age" on a personal level means healing, wholing, growing, transforming, and going beyond or transcending your old limits, your old prejudices, your old angers, and your old escape mechanisms. It means taking a risk to find your own identity and maintaining a deep rather than a superficial sense of well-being, even when the waters get choppy and you seem to be tossed about on the rough waves of life. Through these transitions or passages in your own life, learning to identify with the ocean instead of the waves, so to speak, or, with the sky, instead of the passing clouds puts you in touch with what is real and eternal within you. Reiki is a gift of life, a natural energy-balancing and healing art and science that, in its essence, puts you in touch with your real self.

There is a wonderful Sufi story passed down for centuries

113

which is entertaining, healing, wholing, and enlightening! It goes like this:

> Once there was a powerful king, ruler of many lands, whose position was so great that wise men were his mere employees. Yet, one day, he felt himself confused so he summoned his sages. To them he said: "I do not know the cause, but something impels me to seek a certain ring. This ring will enable me to stabilize my confusion. I must have this ring and it must be one which will make me happy when I am unhappy, and at the same time, it must make me sad when I am happy and look upon it." The wise men consulted each other and threw themselves into deep reflection of the king's request. Finally, they arrived at a decision as to the nature of the ring which would satisfy their king.
> The ring which they designed had inscribed upon it the **words:**

THIS, TOO, WILL PASS

The wholistic paradigm or model is designed to put you in touch with the whole—to include all that is in the cosmos and not to exclude even a particle. A "prescription for wholeness" begins with deciding at this point in your life the direction you want to go and includes being flexible and adaptable as your *process* unfolds in this life.

Tools for transformation are part of your journey. Reiki is a powerful yet gentle, subtle gift of connecting with life-force energy of a higher order than you normally experience in daily life. The Reiki activating-energy process is completely safe and natural. It does not impose or impress energy on you but rather naturally aligns energy within you. With Reiki, you will be applying this natural life-force energy to your *whole* self, simultaneously balancing yourself physically, emotionally, mentally, and spiritually. With Reiki, you are directly tapping and amplifying your only true power—that which lies within you.

When used as instructed, the Reiki technique restores depleted vital energy and balances your energy naturally. Balancing energy on all levels of your being promotes healing, wholing, transformation, and, ultimately, enlightenment. Reiki is a special gift—a unique method designed to put you in touch with and to amplify your inner strength.

One of the ways used by many people each day for activating the power within is by "affirmations"—the power of the spoken word. Affirmations combined with the light-energy of Reiki give you an especially effective and quick way to quiet outer confusion, control scattered energies, and connect *consciously* with your inner strength.

One of the unique features of the Reiki technique is that it can be used along with other techniques such as affirmations or even while doing other activities. An essential aspect of the gift of Reiki is in its natural, universal quality. Doing some of the Reiki head positions combined with saying affirmations such as, "I am whole, I am well, I am free," or "I know and I know that I know," centers you, heals you, wholes you, and enlightens you.

Giving the gift of Reiki to yourself gives light-energy, vital energy to your body—a natural "food" for a natural organism! The Reiki technique is a direct way of having a positive effect on all levels of your being, of promoting and maintaining positive wellness.

It has been said for centuries that love is the best healer and wholer. Love is a quality of the life force, and Reiki is a gift of love. Love is not something you create. It is your true nature. For centuries, you have been reminded by many wise men that you are the light of the world. Reiki is a gift of light-energy that aligns you with your inner, natural integrity. Your hands are a gift through which you can channel and direct this cosmic love, light-energy of Reiki. If for some reason you do not have use of your hands, Reiki can be directed through other parts of your body or being.

In Reiki Seminars, I often refer to Reiki as the gift of the universe or the gift of the cosmos. The Reiki factor has been preserved and passed through the centuries to be rediscovered as a light-energy source now available to all of us as we step into the New Age of humanity and the New Age of ourselves.

In one Reiki class, a woman experienced a deep and profound insight which she shared: "If everyone in the whole world took the Reiki, we would have no more murders—no more wars." In her words, she captured the ultimate gift of Reiki—the gift of life and the gift of honoring the life-force in all of us.

I invite you to take the Reiki Seminar, to give yourself the gift of Reiki, to experience Reiki for yourself, and to incorporate it into your lifestyle in whatever ways are appropriate and special for you. Whatever your age, if you are alive you can learn, grow, and transform. The gift of Reiki is in its putting you in touch with life-force energy and freeing you into the awareness that every day is a new beginning.